A Gymnastic Riding System

using

MIND,

BODY,

& SPIRIT

PROGRESSIVE TRAINING
FOR RIDER AND HORSE

Betsy Steiner

with Jennifer O. Bryant

Foreword by
Klaus Balkenhol

TRAFALGAR SQUARE PUBLISHING

NORTH POMFRET
VERMONT

First published in 2003 by
Trafalgar Square Publishing
North Pomfret, Vermont 05053

Printed in China

Photographs on pages 39, 49, 56, 70–75, 81, 88–89, 113–114, 117–118, 124, 134–150, 142, 146–150, 154–157, 159–160, 176, 178–179, 185–189, 192–193, 202–203, 208, 212, 219, 221–233, 238–239, 247 by Phelpsphotos.com; pages 24, 46–48, 54, 58, 94–96, 99, 108, 129, 132–133, 136–137, 200, 241 by Mandy Lorraine; pages 65, 76–77 by Rhett Savoie.

Disclaimer of Liability

The authors and publisher shall have neither liability nor responsibility to any person or entity with respect to any loss or damage caused or alleged to be caused directly or indirectly by the information contained in this book. While the book is as accurate as the authors can make it, there may be errors, omissions, and inaccuracies.

Library of Congress Cataloging-in-Publication Data

Steiner, Betsy.
  A gymnastic riding system using mind, body, and spirit:
progressive training for rider and horse / Betsy Steiner with Jennifer O. Bryant.
       p. cm.
Includes bibliographical references (p.   ).
  ISBN-13: 978-1-57076-092-1
  ISBN-10: 1-57076-092-6 (hardcover)
1. Horses—Training. 2. Horses—Exercise. I. Bryant, Jennifer O.
(Jennifer Olson) II. Title.

  SF287 .S75 2003
  798.2'3—dc21

                          2002151258

Cover and book design by Carrie Fradkin
Typeface: Cheltenham

Color separations by Tenon & Polert Colour Scanning Ltd.

9 8 7 6 5 4 3

Table of Contents

Dedication

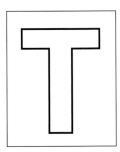

his book is dedicated to my parents, June and Mac McMillan, who made me believe all things are possible. To my daughter Jessie, a beautiful, sensitive rider with a deep love for her horses. She has been my best friend, my right hand, and my best cheerleader and supporter throughout her life— she makes it all worthwhile. Last but not least, to all the wonderful horses who have blessed my life and made it so rich.

Acknowledgments

I have many people to thank for their generosity in helping me write this book. First and foremost is Caroline Robbins for her belief in my concept of the book. Both she and Martha Cook gave me valuable guidance and showed great patience for the time it took to complete this book. I thank Jennifer Bryant for the endless hours spent interviewing me, for her gift of organization and her writing skills. Susan Habanova shared with me her talents and creativity for understanding now to develop the human athlete through her expertise in Pilates. Mary Phelps and JJ Hathaway for all of their photos and fun we had taking them. Many gracious thanks to my friend Mandy Lorraine for her focus as a professional and through the camera lens. Sandy Rabinowitz for her wonderful illustrations, patience, and good humor. Jane Rainis not only dedicated hours of time with her grammatical assistance, analytical mind and sense of joy, but also let me use her lovely horse, Heraut, for photos. My thanks to Jodie Kelly who generously lent me her "ever ready" and wonderful horse, Manhattan, to demonstrate some exercises in the book. To Courtney Budd for her valuable photo shoot assistance. A special thank you to Mary Ann and Walter McPhail for allowing me to use their beautiful showgrounds for the photography. I thank Karen Sakas and Julia Peter for being good sports in trying out new exercises for the book. To Kathy Connelly and Guenter Seidel for their constant friendship and support. My gratitude to Kathie Moehlig for providing years of inspiration. To my good friend Tami Hoag for her literary encouragement, imagination and inspiration, both in writing and riding.

first met Betsy Steiner at the 1990 World Championships held in Stockholm where she admirably represented the United States on her horse, Unanimous. Since that time, I have had the pleasure of coaching her on numerous occasions during United States Equestrian Team and U.S. Dressage Federation clinics, and most recently in my position as official coach for the American team. I am continually impressed with Betsy's ability to ride and train at a very high international standard, and by her innate talent for working quickly and successfully with horses—even ones that are not familiar to her.

It is a great pleasure for me to be able to introduce this wonderful, creative book, which encompasses many of her special attributes as a rider, trainer, and teacher. These qualities include her dedication to horses, training them with great empathy, passion, and humor using the mind, body, and spirit approach that she presents to the reader here; her ability to teach riders at all levels, with her warm, easy-to-approach, encouraging manner; and her strong belief of the importance of the rider being as much of an athlete as the horse—physical fitness being the vital component for riding with an effective seat, and truly light, independent aids.

Many books focus on riding instruction, and others on the training of horses, and nearly all concentrate on the use of the rider's (and the horse's) mind and body to achieve results. Betsy, however, goes one step further, adding a third element—the spiritual side of being. This is the place where, not only the rider's "feel," and empathy for the horse is found, but also where a horse's personality, moods, likes and dislikes are discovered—traits that must be considered by the sensitive, caring rider and trainer since preserving the horse's spirit is one of our major obligations.

This book maps out a marvelous approach to riding, using the classical training pyramid as a base for her mind, body, and spirit system of training. She presents this together with solid, gymnastic, physical advice for both rider and horse, and the result is a unique compilation of all Betsy's best qualities as a horseman. Her love of horses and her kindness as a human being also shine through, and because the reader will be infected by her enthusiasm, as well as influenced by her gentleness and humanity, it is my hope that this book will be read by many.

Klaus Balkenhol
Olympic Team Gold Medalist for Germany in 1992 and 1996
U.S. Dressage Team Coach, 2000 to 2004

Throughout my riding career, I have been taught to develop myself as a rider in the same systematic, patient, methodical way that we develop our horses as athletes and partners. I have had the good fortune to work with some of the modern masters—Christilot Boylen, Egon von Neindorff, Uwe Steiner, Georg Theodorescu, Herbert Rehbein, Guenter Seidel, Klaus Balkenhol, Robert Dover, and Kathy Connelly, to name the ones who have imparted the most to me.

My first serious dressage study was in Canada, at Christilot's farm. I was just seventeen when I became her working student. Christilot's mother, Willy Blok Hansen, had a dance studio, and I took classes twice a week—mostly calisthenics and other exercises that dancers use to stretch and strengthen their muscles and to improve balance and flexibility. As I practiced in the dance studio and in the riding arena, I began to realize that how I moved and used my body had a significant effect on how my horse moved and used *his* body.

The following year, I traveled to Germany and spent a year at Egon von Neindorff's famed Reitinstitut. The most important thing to Von Neindorff was the rider's seat, and I spent about six months on the longe line. His philosophy was simple: If you could not sit, there was no reason for you to touch a rein. So, we longed until my seat bones and knees were raw. I learned that it was essential for me to develop as an athlete and to gain body-awareness if I wanted to have perfect balance in the saddle. The process was both physical and intellectual: My muscles and coordination had to develop, and at the same time I had to gain an under-standing of what I was trying to achieve in my riding and why.

As I learned, I began to figure out how to use my aids to effectively communi-cate to the horse what I wanted—which meant, of course, that I had to thorough-ly understand the purpose and application of each aid. Thanks to my early trainers' insistence that I develop myself as an athlete and take the time to learn the funda-mentals of dressage, I learned to become a more efficient rider. As a petite woman and 5 feet 4 inches tall, efficiency is especially important; I can't influence a horse with weight and leverage the way that a man can.

Because of a burning desire to become the best rider I could be, I became interested in using other methods to improve my fitness and my riding. I was intro-duced to several approaches that have helped me as a rider: in particular, aerobic training, weight training, t'ai chi, yoga, and most important to me now, the *Pilates* Method of body conditioning—the approach to rider athleticism that I have adapt-ed especially for riders, a system I call *Equilates* (see p. 33).

Maintaining proper form and alignment not only produces better results; it also reduces stress on the body and therefore minimizes the risk of injury. This made a huge impact on my own training, and when I discovered that it was true for both human *and* equine athletes, it made a whole lot of sense to train my horses in the same way. My thinking started to be that, if I just use my leg and my horse trots off, I've done nothing to help him align his joints and take off with a good clean stride from behind. The challenge then became, "How do I achieve this?" I realized that the answer is through my own body alignment. If I am perfectly aligned and straight so that no joint is stressed, my horse will find it much easier to follow my body language and naturally fall into that alignment. Then I can use a program of gymnastic exercises to strengthen and supple his muscles so that he can maintain that alignment and balance with ease. Because I am training my own body, I have an insight into the way my horse is feeling as he goes through the training process.

Let's face it: Most people today lead extremely busy lives, with jobs, families, and other commitments. For many riders, it's an accomplishment just to carve out the time to get to the barn and ride—and doing so takes a lot of commitment, organization, diligence, and plain hard work. Some of you may be thinking, "My schedule is already maxed out; I can't possibly squeeze in additional exercises, workout time, or painstaking record keeping."

Fair enough. But what if I told you that if you can set aside just 30 minutes a day, three days a week, you can become a more efficient rider? That those minutes spent on yourself will pay off in less frustration with yourself and your horse, making the experience much more positive and productive, and save you time in the long run? If you're a beginner- or intermediate-level rider, that your sessions could cease to be a struggle to gain mastery over your own body in the saddle and that you'll begin to discover the ease, grace, and elegance of a riding position that's in proper balance and alignment? Or, if you're an advanced rider, that you'll unearth even deeper layers of discovery about your relationship with your horse and ever-subtler (and more effective) means of communicating with him?

You may be thinking, the time investment sounds like a "win-win." But what about the financial investment? Do I have to join a pricey health club or buy expensive equipment? Not at all! All you need to do the unmounted *Pilates* exercises in this book is comfortable clothing that allows free range of movement and a space that's large enough to sit and stretch out in. If you find that you enjoy the exercises and want to do and learn more, by all means seek the guidance of a reputable *Pilates* or *Equilates* fitness professional and add some equipment to your workouts (for help, log on to www.pilates-studio.com, or www.equilates.com). But for the purposes of this book, you need not purchase any special equipment or enroll in a program—and if you travel a lot, you'll be especially glad that many of the exercises are uncomplicated and easy to do in a hotel room.

A Word About Your Health

As with any exercise program, consult your physician before you begin any new fitness activity. I especially urge pregnant women to refrain from embarking on new forms of exercise until they get a doctor's approval. (And if you're pregnant, talk to your doctor about whether it's okay for you to continue riding.)

The approach and exercises in this book generally require too much focus, coordination, and discipline for children under the age of twelve. Young children can and do enjoy ponies and riding, but such a comprehensive program may require more commitment (and seem like more work) than they're capable of taking on at this age.

Whatever your age, fitness level, or health status, please use common sense as you experiment with the exercises in this book. If something hurts, stop and check with your doctor. Don't overdo, and introduce new movements and concepts slowly—just as you would with your horse. As in dressage, form, balance, and alignment are key. This means that three repetitions of an exercise, done in proper form, are far more beneficial than ten or fifteen done incorrectly. What's more, sloppy form puts you at greater risk of injury.

Enjoy the Journey

There are many wonderful "how to" books written, but if you're like many riders, you've read other books on riding and horsemanship—even those written by some of the great masters—and struggled to put their advice and philosophies into practice. My aim in writing this book was to help bridge the gap between the many excellent equestrian texts and the practical application of their teachings. After all, how can a rider do what the masters advise if he or she is not physically able or mentally prepared to do so?

My goal in creating this book is to make it eminently usable. This isn't a textbook that you read in your living room and then shelve. Instead, I hope that you'll find the concepts, exercises, and goal-setting directions exciting and practical enough that you'll take this book with you to the barn and perhaps keep it in your tack trunk for review, encouragement, and inspiration.

Most of all, I hope that reading and using this book improves the quality and pleasure of your daily work with your horse. I wish you the joys of discovery and kinship as you establish a connection—not just in your riding, but in your life.

CHAPTER ONE

A *Mind-Body-Spirit* **APPROACH**

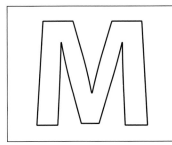ost books on dressage discuss the *physical* aspects of riding: horse position, rider position, purpose and use of the aids, schooling exercises, and movements. But, in my opinion, the *physical* (body) is just one-third of the riding equation. There are two remaining thirds—the *intellectual* (mind), and the *psychological* (spirit), which are just as important as the physical mechanics of riding. My approach to riding and training horses is to use the body, mind, *and* spirit. They all need to work together, and if you have only concentrated on the mechanics of riding, you have not availed yourself of two-thirds of the process. In this book, I will give you these other two-thirds, and I'll show you how to tie them together with the first third to create a richness of experience with your horse.

When you look in the mirror, do you see your entire self—mind, body, and spirit? No. All you can see is your physical being—your body. Your physical self is an important part of who you are, and its state of health, fitness, and vigor has a great deal to do with how you feel about yourself and about life in general. But you are much more than a physical entity. You also have a mind that is uniquely your own. Your thoughts, opinions, intellectual aptitudes, and learning processes are different from anyone else's. And, you have a spirit—a psyche—that is just as distinctive. Your emotions and psychological makeup, which are shaped in part by genetics and in part by your life experiences, are like no one else's. Think about the complex combination of your unique body, mind, and spirit, and it's easy to see why no two people perceive the world in exactly the same way.

Gymnastic training, by definition a training system that starts at the bottom and moves up a ladder to achieve a higher level, enables you to become athletic, lithe, energetic, supple, and flexible. But, *gymnastic training* is not just a *physical* activity. To explain, let me give you a musical analogy about becoming a complete pianist: You must first learn a specific physical technique in order play a basic scale on the piano. Then you must be able to master a simple tune before you can play a complicated piece. Finally, you will need to completely understand the music and *feel* it in your soul, before you can perform it with emotion, and move an audience. And so it is with training and riding—you need your body, mind, and spirit—to achieve the ultimate.

Some people may think otherwise, but I believe that animals also possess a "mind" and a "spirit" element. Your horse is not simply a physical being; he's a thinking, feeling creature with a unique personality and set of physical *and* mental strengths and weaknesses. What's more, horses can and do have profound effects on humans. I believe that the horse is one of God's purest forms. He is a remarkably complex being—an extraordinary blending of strength and power with kindness, gentleness, and innocence. All horses are born with these qualities. Horses that possess all of these innate attributes *plus* talent become a metaphor for what we humans aspire to: a perfect balance of mind, body, and spirit—plus a little something special.

If you doubt that horses can function on such a sophisticated level of awareness and understanding, think about the times when you've seen, as I have, a horse who would buck off an experienced rider yet stands quietly under a squealing, wiggling child, or a horse who takes extra care with a handicapped rider or a frail elderly person. How does the horse know that he shouldn't indulge in his usual antics? It isn't because somebody told him. Rather, it's because he possesses a keen sensitivity and a sort of sixth sense about our physical and emotional states.

My philosophies have led me to create a training system that addresses the rider as well as the horse, and that addresses both as the three-dimensional beings that they are.

How to Use This Book

I have based *A Gymnastic Riding System* on the *Classical Training Pyramid* for horses as defined by the German National Equestrian Federation, and as published in the U.S. Dressage Federation Manual. The *Classical Training Pyramid* comprises six levels, each level consisting of a component that represents a critical rung of the training ladder. Just as a house must be built on a solid foundation, a horse must achieve a certain degree of mastery at each level before he can truly embark on the next—although expert trainers can and do school aspects of neighboring levels at one time.

My system consists of two brand new pyramids. I call them the **Rider's** *Mind-Body-Spirit Training Building Blocks*; and the **Horse's** *Mind-Body-Spirit Training Building Blocks*. They correspond to the *Classical Training Pyramid*, but are my own pyramids of training to develop all *three* facets of rider and horse—the intellectual or knowledge aspect; the physical; and the spiritual or psychological.

All the chapters that follow this one, will be named for, and focus on, the six individual components of the *Classical Training Pyramid*. Starting at the bottom rung, the components are: *Rhythm, Suppleness, Contact, Impulsion, Straightness,* and *Collection*. In each chapter, I will define the component, explain its importance in *gymnastic training*, and present my rider and horse *Mind-Body-Spirit Building Blocks* for the component under discussion. I show you how to set realistic, attainable goals for yourself and your horse; and I'll give you one or more exercises that you can use to improve your skills. I'll also show you how to assess your progress and evaluate whether it's time to move on to the next level. Finally, I'll give you some easy tips to aid your understanding as you work on that particular component.

So, in order to begin, and to understand where *A Gymnastic Riding System* is going to take you, your riding, and your relationship with your horse, you need to have a basic knowledge of the *Classical Training Pyramid* (fig. 1.1). This tried-and-true system for training a horse to become an all-around athlete works by starting with rhythm and tempo, and weaving into suppleness and contact. Once these are established, the horse is physically and mentally prepared to move into impulsion, true straightness, and finally collection and self-carriage. Because you are dealing with a living being, this can take some time—many years in most cases. Every horse needs to move forward at his own pace and it is the rider's responsibility to be sensitive and react to what her horse needs, advancing him when he is ready.

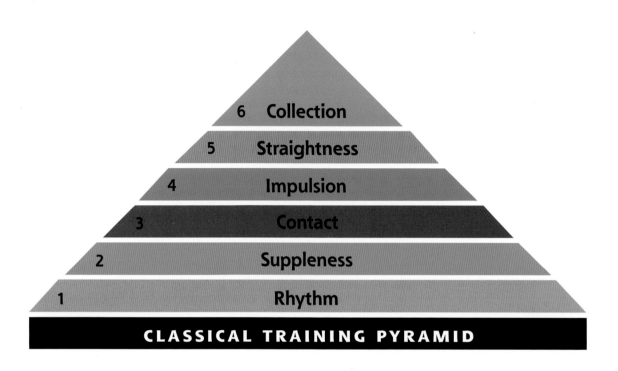

1.1

The Classical Training Pyramid

Of course, for countless different reasons, many a horse will never achieve the physical attributes necessary for the uppermost levels of the pyramid. However, that does not mean that he and you will not benefit from the information I impart at those levels, because much of it applies to horses in general—evaluating their contentment, for instance—and the rider's building blocks at every level (the rider has an obligation to develop as an athlete in order to become an equal partner) can be followed by all, no matter what level of gymnastic development their horse is performing at. And, remember, even if your horse cannot perform one of the "body" elements at a particular level, he may well be ready for a "spirit" building block. This training system is meant to be three-dimensional. Just remember that it takes time to develop muscles, and time for the mind to comprehend how to ask the body to flow with grace and ease.

The *Pyramid*—wide and solid at its base, its lines converging at the structure's peak—is a visual metaphor for the process of *gymnastically training* a horse by using the classical methods. The levels of the training pyramid build, one upon the other, until the horse reaches the ultimate stage in his athletic and psychological development. Here is an introduction to the levels and the skills that they encompass, starting at the beginning.

Rhythm: Regular, even, steady, cadenced paces.

Suppleness: Ability to bend the body both laterally and longitudinally; looseness; fluidity.

Contact: Acceptance of the bit and the rider's hands; willingness to go forward into the bit; connection of the haunches to the forehand.

Impulsion: Propulsive, or "pushing," power-packed energy from the hindquarters; development of energy; loading of energy onto power-packed, spring-like joints.

Straightness: Sophisticated and correctly trained alignment of the body on straight and curved lines.

Collection: Moving in self-carriage (the horse's body is developed in such a way to move, balance, and be harmonious with, not opposed to, the rider's body) with the strides showing increased suspension and "air time" through increased bending of the joints, particularly of the hindquarters and the hind legs.

It is important to realize that, even when a horse has reached the uppermost level of the *Training Pyramid*, he is not necessarily "finished," with nothing more to learn. All of the most successful international-level riders school their Grand Prix horses regularly on the basics, to continue to develop their ability to carry themselves and to hone their mastery of every component of the *Training Pyramid*. The building-block approach of the *Pyramid* represents an ongoing dynamic process with ever-deepening layers, not a finite course of study with a beginning, middle, and end.

Introduction to the Mind-Body-Spirit Training Building Blocks

The first thing you'll notice about the *Mind-Body-Spirit Training Building Blocks* is that there are two of them: one for the *rider*, and one for the *horse* (fig. 1.2). As I said earlier, this is because I believe that training involves two athletes—not just the horse—and that those two athletes each have an intellect, a physical body, and a unique psychological makeup. It goes without saying that horses' and humans' bodies are different, that we see the world differently than our horses do, and that we have different kinds of intellect. Therefore, it's impossible to chart your training progression and your horse's according to the same standards. However, there will

MIND	BODY	SPIRIT

THE RIDER

MIND	BODY	SPIRIT
6 Total Psychological Self-Control	6 Total Body Control	6 Focus
5 Positioning	5 Alignment	5 Commitment
4 Energy	4 Core Strength with Power	4 Enthusiasm & Excitement
3 Connection	3 Coordination	3 Consistency & Steadiness
2 Purpose of Aids	2 Flexibility	2 Relaxation & Flow
1 Tempo & Footfalls	1 Strength	1 Patience

THE HORSE

MIND	BODY	SPIRIT
6 Total Balance	6 Self-carriage	6 Focus
5 Body Awareness	5 Alignment	5 Contentment
4 Power & Activity	4 Energy	4 Electric
3 Forward within Connection	3 Balance	3 Trust & Confidence
2 Yields to the Leg	2 Fluency & Flexibility	2 Willingness
1 Leg Equals Forward	1 Strength	1 Obedience & Work Ethic

MBS TRAINING BUILDING BLOCKS

1.2

The Mind-Body-Spirit
Training Building Blocks
for Rider and Horse

be times that you discover your horse ahead of you and you can learn from him, whereas other times, you are his teacher.

The second thing you will have noticed about the *Mind-Body-Spirit Building Blocks* is that, unlike the *Classical Training Pyramid*, they are three-dimensional. Many of the books on dressage are written as if riders use only their intellect, and horses use only their bodies. The three-dimensional nature of the *Building Blocks* also reflects the fact that mind, body, and spirit, for the most part, develop together.

I always address the *rider's* development first, and then the *horse's*. That's because you, as the rider, are the leading partner in the dance: You're in control of what happens to your own body and, therefore, you have the ability to influence your horse's. But your responsibility goes even deeper than that. In truth, you control practically everything that happens to your horse, from where he lives and what he eats to what he does for a living. It's an enormous responsibility, being in charge of another living creature that depends on you for its survival. So, by addressing the rider issues first, I'm reminding you that you can almost always look to yourself first to find the answers to any problems or questions you may encounter during your training.

Horses are a reflection of their riders. A stiff rider will produce a stiff horse. A rider who cannot control her position will never be able to position her horse effectively. If you cannot use your seat, you will find that your horse's haunches don't truly engage. In most cases, you can look at a rider's position and see that position reflected in the horse's body. There's another reason that I've chosen to address the rider first in my discussions: You can trade your horse in for another one, but you can't trade yourself. So if you don't start with yourself, it doesn't matter how many times you trade horses. You have to focus on getting yourself in order. As the rider, you can create the results that you want.

Coming next in this chapter, I am going to give you a quick overview of the elements of the rider's and horse's *Mind-Body-Spirit Training Building Blocks* that correspond to the six components of the *Classical Training Pyramid*. I will be discussing all these elements in the chapters that follow, and for easy reference have given you the page numbers ahead so you can find the complete discussion in greater detail.

The **RIDER'S** Mind-Body-Spirit Training Building Blocks
An Overview

Rider's **Building Block 1:** RHYTHM

Intellectual element: Tempo and footfalls

Athletic element: Strength

Psychological element: Patience

Mind: To be able to develop rhythm in your horse, you must first understand what rhythm is. You also must understand the sequence of footfalls in each gait—the "one, two, three, four" of the walk, the "one-two, one-two" of the trot, and the "one-two-three" of the canter. You need to be able to see, feel, and hear the patterns of footfalls and to recognize when they're irregular or at an inappropriate tempo (too fast or too slow) for your horse's way of going and for the pace desired.

Body: To be able to sit on a horse and use your aids to start, stop, and steer him, you must possess a certain amount of body strength. If you lack even basic muscle tone, you'll have difficulty maintaining your balance atop a moving animal. Your legs may not be strong enough to give the aid to your horse to move forward or sideways, and your arms and hands may lack the muscular development to hold and use the reins to get the results you want.

Spirit: Above all else, working with horses takes patience. You may be the most gifted rider and trainer in history; but if you get frustrated easily or lose your temper, you'll get nowhere fast. You also need to have patience with yourself—to at first forgive yourself for making mistakes, and later to move into a place where there are no "mistakes" but only opportunities to learn, and not to give up when you hit a training plateau or struggle with a concept that doesn't come easily. (For more on RHYTHM, see p. 27.)

Rider's **Building Block 2:** SUPPLENESS

Intellectual element: Purpose of aids

Athletic element: Flexibility

Psychological element: Relaxation and flow

Mind: In riding, suppling and bending work usually takes the form of various gymnastic exercises, such as serpentines and shoulder-in. Leading a horse through these exercises requires you to use a complex combinations of aids—leg, seat, and hands. Before you can give these aids correctly and with appropriate timing and intensity, you need to understand what the aids are and how they influence the horse.

Body: A stiff rider cannot produce a relaxed, supple horse, so you need to develop flexibility in your own muscles and joints. You need to be able to feel that flexibility in your own body before you can experience it in your horse's body. One of the goals of *gymnastic training* is to produce a horse that is equally supple and strong on both sides; likewise, you may need to work to overcome your "sidedness" (thought to be caused mostly by our being right- or left-handed) in order to develop equilateral flexibility.

Spirit: Part of being supple is having a supple body; the other part is having a calm, relaxed mind—one that has a certain amount of willingness to "go with the flow." A rider who brings a demanding, rigid, angry, or fearful mindset to the arena is almost guaranteed to engender similar resistance in the horse. (For more on SUPPLENESS, see p. 63.)

Rider's Building Block 3: CONTACT
Intellectual element: Connection
Athletic element: Coordination
Psychological element: Consistency and steadiness

Mind: It is at this point in the training progression of levels that rider and horse alike have to make a big jump in their intellectual understanding as well as in their physical development. "Contact" is a complex concept, one that requires you to develop an understanding of the idea that your horse must learn to accept contact with the bit while continuing to go forward in response to your seat and legs.

Body: When he does so, he is said to be "connected"—allowing the energy created by using his abdominal muscles to activate his hindquarters so that they flow forward over his topline, up to his poll, and into the rider's hands, then back down, through his neck, and along his abdominal muscles and back to his haunches, where the "circle of the aids" or "muscle ring" begins anew. Creating and channeling this energy takes skillful riding and coordination of the aids, and doing so requires keen body awareness to enable total body coordination on your part. You'll need to work to develop excellent timing, as well as the ability to use different parts of your body at the same time, in order to activate the muscle ring that will encourage your horse to accept contact and connection.

Spirit: Because the concepts and exercises at this stage can get complicated, it's easy for riders to get flustered or even not to realize that their aids are "off-again, on-again" or varying in their intensity. Consistency and steadiness are the key words here—not only in your body and your aids, but also in your frame of mind. Even if your horse struggles or resists in confusion or because he feels overwhelmed, you stay calm and steady, your demeanor and your aids telling him, "*Here* is where I'd like for you to be." (For more on CONTACT, see p. 110.)

Rider's **Building Block 4:** IMPULSION

> Intellectual element: Energy
> Athletic element: Core strength with power
> **Psychological element:** Enthusiasm and excitement

Impulsion is "forward with pizzazz." It's power-packed "pushing power." Watching a horse move with real impulsion, you get the feeling of stored—almost explosive—energy, and a sense that he could easily accelerate, collect, or change direction at a moment's notice.

Mind: To create impulsion in your horse, you first have to understand the concept of energy—that it's stored and controlled, not expended flat-out. Your horse's hindquarters store energy like a coiled spring, and that energy can similarly be unleashed with the merest movement on your part.

Even more than your legs, your seat is the aid that creates impulsion in your horse. As I'll discuss in more detail in Chapter Five, the "seat" is really the rider's abdomen and back. Fitness trainers often refer to this part of the anatomy as the "core," and *Pilates* trainers (more on *Pilates* on p. 34) call it the "powerhouse," but whatever you call it, it is the most important part of your body as a rider. Your upper and lower legs work in harmony and support of your seat . Unfortunately, many fitness regimens and forms of exercise strengthen the core only to a limited extent. Weight lifters, for instance, may spend hours sculpting their arms, shoulders, and legs but (save for the obsession for the coveted abdominal "six-pack" look) pay little attention to strengthening the deep "core" muscles of the torso.

Body: Energy also affects your degree of balance. The lines of energy in your body are related to your degree of "core stability." A rider with core stability has energy (and movement) in her hips yet has a seemingly motionless upper body. Many riders, however, try to get the job done with too much upper-body movement—which prevents their horses from becoming engaged. If a rider rocks her upper body forward in a flying change, for instance, her horse's croup usually comes up, meaning that she, through her body language, has allowed him to lose the engagement.

Spirit: Impulsion and energy are positive, "up" states of body and mind. When I want to create impulsion in a horse, I get excited—literally. I feel a surge of enthusiasm and excitement. I get "jazzed." I feel happy. It's hard for me to imagine trying to create impulsion in a horse while my mind is dull and tired. As is so true with every aspect of riding, I must create in myself the mental and physical state that I would like for my horse to follow. (For more on IMPULSION, see p. 144.)

Rider's Building Block 5: STRAIGHTNESS

Intellectual element: Positioning
Athletic element: Alignment
Psychological element: Commitment

Mind: The term "straightness" is misleading to many riders because it conjures up an image of a horse that's straight as a board from head to tail, all the time. In truth, horses can't be straight as boards because their hindquarters are wider than their forehands. Left to their own devices, most horses travel slightly haunches-in or shoulders-out. But for the inside hind leg to step up underneath the body, thereby causing the horse to carry more weight over his hindquarters and to take a loftier stride, he must bring his shoulders in line with or slightly ahead of his haunches. When he does this, we say that he is straight, and we actually mean that he is correctly aligned. That's how a horse can be said to be "straight" on a circle. He is aligned, with both his shoulders and his haunches on the curve of the circle, and his body bent to conform to the circle's arc.

It may seem strange that straightness comes so high up in the *Training Pyramid.* You may ask yourself, "Don't I need to be straight to find my *rhythm* and *tempo*?" The answer is yes. Of course, it's important to keep your horse as straight as possible (as defined above) right from the beginning. But the straightness I am talking about in this *Building Block* can be likened to the discipline, training, and precise balance of a prima ballerina, as compared to a dancer just beginning her career. Through classical principles, the prima ballerina has developed a depth to her body carriage and alignment. This enables her to become perfectly straight, and move effortlessly from movement to movement with grace and elegance. Both dancers develop their skill from the same ballet positions, it's just that through the experience of practice, one dancer develops a depth that is reflected in the confidence and precision of her movement.

Body: In order for your horse to be straight, you must be straight, or correctly aligned. If your weight is not distributed evenly in the saddle, from your hips and through both legs, with your torso erect, you will throw your horse off balance. If you inadvertently carry one arm tensed or one hand higher than the other, you will exert a constant pull on one rein, and your horse's neck and head will always tend to bend in that direction. If you sit crookedly, with one hip ahead of the other and one shoulder higher than the other, you will cause your horse to carry himself the same way to compensate for your imbalance. You may even want to ask yourself, for instance: "Is that why he's always late in that flying change?" and to check to see if it's *you* who's late with *your* hip.

Spirit: Finally, at this stage of training, your spirit—your psychological mind-set—must be one of commitment. It takes many horses and riders years to reach this stage of training, and so of course they've already demonstrated a considerable amount of commitment. But riding at this level is exacting and demanding, and achieving *true* straightness (as opposed to "straightness" on a line or curve as necessary in the earlier levels) isn't a "halfway" endeavor. Your horse is either straight or he's not. Maintaining straightness—aligning him through his *entire* body all the time, through every corner for every step—requires constant adjustment. Are you willing to keep at it—and to work to overcome your own natural imbalances—not only to bring your body into harmonious action, but also to influence your horse's alignment and harmony? (For more on STRAIGHTNESS, see p. 180.)

Rider's **Building Block 6:** COLLECTION

Intellectual element: Total psychological self-control
Athletic element: Total body control
Psychological element: Focus

Collection is the top rung on the dressage-training ladder. A collected horse moves with the ultimate degree of controlled power and suspension of which he is capable. Ideally, he maintains his balance, alignment, and cadence with little assistance from the rider, and so he is said to go in "self-carriage."

Mind: To achieve this state of peak performance, the rider must create a highly honed and attuned mind, body, and spirit. Intellectually, you need the confidence that your knowledge of the philosophies, theories, and applications of equestrian technique is sufficient to enable you to lead your horse-rider partnership confidently and successfully. In other words, you know what to do, and you have the tools to handle any situation that may arise. Although you continually strive to hone your skills and to develop new levels of understanding, you are not struggling to understand concepts, or trying to learn "feel" or timing for the first time.

Body: Likewise, to reach this level you must have achieved a high degree of mastery over your own body. Not only do you need to be fit, strong, and flexible; you also need to be able to use your body to influence your horse's, and to use your seat, legs, and hands independent of one another. Body awareness is key, and you must be able to engage certain muscles while others are relaxed, that is muscles working independently of each other so that you can drive with your seat but relax with your arms.

Spirit: Last, and perhaps most important, you need to be able to focus completely on the task at hand—to shut out distractions, pressures, nerves, and worries and to enter what sport psychologists call a "flow state" or a state of peak performance. An athlete who is "in the zone" is in a state of maximal adrenaline flow combined with relaxation—sufficiently "up" to be able to produce a good performance, yet mentally and physically calm enough not to make nervous mistakes or to become exhausted prematurely. All of this requires constant attention and solid training. During training, one facet of the mind-body-spirit balance may be stronger than another. The ideal is when all three elements confidently blend together. (For more on COLLECTION, see p. 215.)

Summary

Incorporate the *Building Blocks* that you have learned into each new *Building Block* you move into. This way you have the foundation of the first *Building Block*, which you then build on, increasing the difficulty, but never compromising the consistency with which you weave each step into the next.

In the chapters that follow, I'll discuss each of the *Rider's Training Building Blocks* and their intellectual, physical, and psychological components in detail.

Then I'll give you exercises and strategies so that you can work on each one. But first, let's preview the six *Classical Training Pyramid* components as they relate to my *Mind-Body-Spirit Training Building Blocks* for your partner, the *horse*.

The **HORSE'S** Mind-Body-Spirit Training Building Blocks
An Overview

Before I start, I'd like to take a moment to again address the doubts or concerns of those readers who are thinking that the idea of a horse having a "spiritual" side is implausible at best or downright "New-Age-y" at worst. I believe that there's nothing strange or "touchy-feely" about taking your horse's personality, moods, quirks, likes, and dislikes into consideration as you work with him; in fact, I believe that it would be impractical *not* to do so. In truth, it is nothing new to talk about a horse's spirit; many of the great masters of equitation have written about the importance of preserving the horse's spirit and keeping him a happy, healthy partner.

As you "tune in" to your own body and mind over the course of the exercises and programs in this book, you may find that you begin to develop greater sympathy for your horse's behaviors as he goes to work each day. If you don't have prior experience doing strength training, say, you may not be acquainted with the muscle awareness and fatigue that can follow a strenuous workout. If your physical activity consists mainly of riding and you don't follow a supplementary workout regimen, you may have less sympathy for occasional resistance on your horse's part caused by a simple case of "Oh, not again!" burnout or boredom.

Perhaps most important, developing a greater understanding of the way your horse thinks and feels will make you a better horseman. You will be better able to discern whether resistance is caused by playfulness, pain, fear, confusion, or simply a little naughtiness. You will learn what makes your horse "tick"—whether he's essentially eager or lazy, brave or timid, polite or assertive, and whether he'd rather be galloping and jumping, dancing in a dressage arena, or meandering over the trails. You may spare him needless (albeit unintended) suffering, and you may spare yourself frustration and heartache. In short, you may make both your lives easier and happier.

I'll be discussing these points more in later chapters. For now, though, I hope you're convinced enough (or at least intrigued enough) that we can go on with our preview of the horse's training progression.

***Horse's* Building Block 1:** RHYTHM

    Knowledge element: Leg equals "forward"

    Athletic element: Strength

    Psychological element: Obedience and work ethic

Mind: Before your horse can do his own version of "I've got rhythm," he has to be in motion. And before you can put him in motion, you have to teach him to go forward from your aid, and that aid is your seat and legs. Many of us have been riding for so long that we've forgotten that horses aren't born knowing that a push from the seat or a kick from the legs means "go forward" and that additional pushes or kicks mean "accelerate to a faster speed or gait." Automatic as the aid may be to us, it doesn't seem to have been instilled quite so thoroughly in many horses. When I teach clinics, the most common training problem I encounter is horses that are not quick enough and insensitive to the leg, or that ignore the leg altogether. As you can see by this component's placement at the foundation of the training scale, "forward from the leg" is the first commandment of *gymnastic training*. Without an understanding of the signal to go forward, you have no foundation for further training, no matter how strong, supple, and elegant your horse may be.

Body: To be able to travel at all three gaits while carrying the weight of a rider and balancing himself accordingly, your horse must possess a certain amount of basic strength, in much the same way that you need a certain amount of basic strength to sit in the saddle and maintain your position. Because we are so much smaller and lighter than horses, it's easy for us to forget just how challenging it can be for them to carry us. Granted, horses are large, impressive-looking animals even at a very young age; but we need to give their bones, joints, and soft tissues time to grow and strengthen before we impose the additional stresses of carrying us.

Spirit: Psychologically, the most fundamental quality to seek is an innately obedient nature or willingness to please, combined with a strong work ethic. True, many outstanding horses have strong personalities and even can be a bit naughty if not handled expertly and sympathetically. Still, a horse that is truly lazy by nature, or that has no interest in developing a working relationship with humans, probably is not destined for a successful performance career. (For more on RHYTHM, see p. 44.)

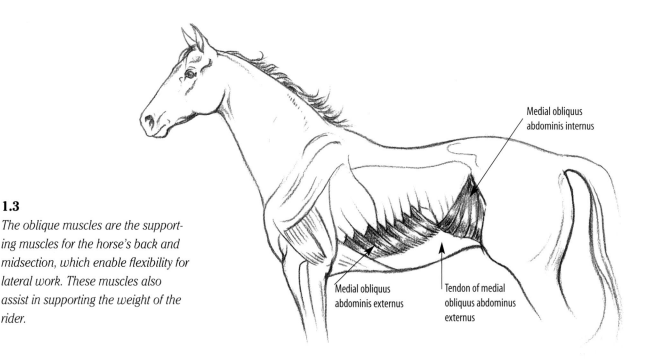

1.3

The oblique muscles are the supporting muscles for the horse's back and midsection, which enable flexibility for lateral work. These muscles also assist in supporting the weight of the rider.

Medial obliquus abdominis internus

Medial obliquus abdominis externus

Tendon of medial obliquus abdominus externus

Horse's **Building Block 2:** SUPPLENESS

    Knowledge element: Yields to the leg
    Athletic element: Fluency and flexibility
    Psychological element: Willingness

Mind: At this stage of training, your horse needs to learn that there are two kinds of leg aids: forward and sideways. He already knows that he must go forward from the leg. Now, your job is to teach him that he must step forward *and* sideways or "yield" when you use one leg more strongly than the other. This understanding forms the foundation of all lateral work: leg-yielding, half-pass, pirouettes, and even flying changes. It keeps the horse supple through his midsection. When he crosses over with a hind leg and steps underneath his haunches, he uses his oblique muscles, which will give him the support he needs to become more supple (fig. 1.3).

Body: Your horse's muscles and joints must be flexible and supple in order for him to move forward and sideways in a flowing, fluent fashion. Lots of gymnastic work and bending exercises will develop his ability to contract his muscles on one side and stretch them on the other.

Spirit: It is a fact that a willingness to work and an eagerness to please can—and often does—compensate for merely average talent. Willingness goes beyond obedience in that it is more than acquiescence to your requests. A willing horse not only agrees to do as you ask; he *wants* to do as you ask. If his heart truly isn't in his work, there will always be an element of "making him do it" in your training sessions—and such a mindset makes it a challenge to produce the kind of brilliance and harmony that marks a truly great equestrian partnership. Willingness creates a joy that is apparent. (For more on SUPPLENESS, see p. 85.)

Horse's Building Block 3: CONTACT

Knowledge element: Forward within connection

Athletic element: Balance

Psychological element: Trust and confidence

Mind: As I mentioned on page 9, the "contact" building block is a critical one in your horse's gymnastic development because it requires a big leap in understanding and physical skill. The critical knowledge at this phase is the concept that he can (and should) go forward willingly, even though you maintain contact with, or a connection to his mouth. Ridden correctly, "connection" is *not* "driving with one foot on the gas pedal and the other on the brake," although some horses tend to back off the contact at first before they learn that they must travel into and "through" it and to allow the rider's hands to help recycle the forward energy through their bodies.

Body: Physically, your horse's balance becomes important as you work to develop contact and connection. At this stage of training, he is learning literally to carry himself in a different way, and he's having to shift his center of gravity back toward his hindquarters and to adjust his balance accordingly. He is developing longitudinal (back to front) balance as well as lateral (side to side) balance through the use of gymnastic exercises such as transitions between gaits, shoulder-in, circles, and half-halts.

Spirit: All of these demands are a lot for a horse to digest, so he needs to feel confident that you, his rider, will not ask him to do anything that's beyond his physical or psychological capability. If he doesn't trust you, or if he lacks confidence in his own ability to do the work, he may respond to the training demands by becoming fearful or resistant. (For more on CONTACT, see p. 126.)

Horse's **Building Block 4:** IMPULSION
> Knowledge element: Power and activity
> Athletic element: Energy
> **Psychological element:** Electric

Mind: Some horses have trouble learning to extend or collect their strides with uplifted power because they don't understand that they have an option other than simply going faster or slower. For your horse to develop impulsion—needed for the extended and collected gaits and as well as a host of other movements—he must first learn to work within the connection you've developed and, therefore, to respond to your aids by making his strides powerful and more lofty, with more suspension or "air time." He must learn to move with dynamic power and activity, not simply speed.

Body: To move with power and activity, your horse must be capable of generating, storing, and releasing great quantities of physical energy. The energy demands of *gymnastic training* are much like those for a human gymnast. A gymnast works for a relatively short period of time, during which he or she alternately displays great muscular control and explodes with power, speed, and lift. It is not likely that a gymnast would be able to run a marathon, or that a marathon runner would be able to perform a gymnastics routine, due to their different muscular and aerobic development. Like the gymnast, your horse needs to develop the ability to direct his energy in a controlled manner and also to "explode" with power when you ask.

Spirit: On page 10, I discussed the way that the rider needs to generate a current of enthusiasm and excitement in order to create impulsion in the horse. Likewise, your horse needs to become "electric"—not nervous and high-strung, but rather sensitive and eager. An "electric" horse is "hot off the leg." He's fun! He doesn't panic or blow up, but he reacts instantly to a very light aid.

It's important to think about creating energy when you ride, starting with the first time you sit on a horse. As you progress, you develop and lift the lines of energy—the "currents," if you will—that run through your horse's body. I see energy in a horse as having three levels of "wattage":

1.4
When you think of impulsion, imagine a ball bouncing your horse up and off the ground.

Low-level energy: The line of energy is on the ground and runs down by the horse's feet. The horse seems to step into the ground as he walks, trots, and canters.

Mid-level energy: As the horse develops better balance, tempo, and contact, the line of energy goes through the middle of his body, to his mouth. He has learned to move into the rider's hands, and he appears to step over the ground.

High-level energy: The energy comes over the horse's entire topline, from his back to his poll. The line of energy now travels from his tail, over his back and neck, and reaches into the rider's hands. To envision this line of energy, imagine holding the ends of a whip in each hand and then moving your hands closer together. The whip will bend upward in the shape of a rainbow, similar to the line of energy in a collected horse. Another way to imagine the line of energy is to imagine bouncing a ball underneath your horse's belly (fig. 1.4). As the ball bounces, he tucks his tummy up and lifts his back, thereby lifting the line of energy. He now looks as though he bounces off the ground! (For more on IMPULSION, see p.164.)

Horse's **Building Block 5:** STRAIGHTNESS

Knowledge element: Body awareness

Athletic element: Alignment

Psychological element: Contentment

Mind: To become straight (aligned), your horse must develop a keen sense of body awareness. Have you ever watched a horse that gives the distinct impression that he cannot keep out of his own way? This is a horse that's lacking body awareness. Balance is an important component of body awareness, but body awareness goes beyond balance. A horse with body awareness is very clear in his understanding of where the different parts of his body are. He has learned through the repetitive reminders from his rider to "tuck your haunches under," "don't drop your shoulder," and so forth. These reminders draw the horse's attention to concentrating on and becoming aware of his balance with each step.

Body: On the physical level, your horse must learn to move in proper alignment in order to become straight. If he is unevenly developed laterally, he will be unable to position or carry himself correctly. If he is out of alignment because of a physical abnormality or developmental defect, or simply because he has a muscle knot or a spinal subluxation, he will be unable to become straight. Your job at this stage of training is to figure out the cause of any crookedness and to take steps to correct those that are fixable, with chiropractic or massage treatments or with other means.

Spirit: The work at this stage of training is challenging, and not all horses have the physical or the psychological makeup needed to reach this level. As I've discussed, your horse's willingness to work and eagerness to please you are important components to your success as partners. At this stage of training, you'd also like for him to seem eager and content with his work and with his role as your partner. Contentment is a quiet confidence—a sense of satisfaction with his lot in life. (For more on STRAIGHTNESS, see p. 198.)

***Horse's* Building Block 6:** COLLECTION
    Knowledge element: Total balance
    Athletic element: Self-carriage
    Psychological element: Focus

Mind: Here we are again at the pinnacle of the training pyramid. Because of each step of the training process, your horse is fully aware of how to move his body. In order for him to succeed at this advanced level, he must develop a complete understanding of how to use his body seemingly effortlessly to remain in balance. Like you, he knows his job, he understands your aids, he is in control of his body, and he's confident that he and you are "speaking the same language."

Body: Self-carriage is the ultimate aim of dressage training. If your horse is in self-carriage, he is in total balance and is able to maintain his rhythm, suppleness, connection, impulsion, and straightness in concert with a rider who possesses the same qualities. At its purest, self-carriage is a deep understanding and experience by both horse and rider of the thoroughness of training. It is "lightness" because every part of the horse's and rider's bodies have been thoroughly connected.

Spirit: Like you, your horse must be very focused at this stage—no looking at other horses or being easily distracted. It may seem funny to you to think of a horse's being "in the zone," but he too must concentrate 100 percent on his work at this level in order to be successful. This is very apparent when you observe the focus of the horses at the Olympic level. They are enormously focused and interested in their job. (For more on COLLECTION, see p. 237.)

An Interactive Process

Now that you've been introduced to the ideas and concepts that we'll be exploring in more detail in the chapters to come, I'd like to give you a few hints on getting the most out of this book.

First, remember: *A Gymnastic Riding System* is like a workbook. As you'll see, each of the following chapters has a format: brief definition and overview of that training building block, followed by a detailed breakdown of how that building block corresponds with the mind-body-spirit components, first for the rider and then for the horse. In each "component" section, you'll find:

▸ Explanation and examples.
▸ Guidelines for setting realistic goals for yourself and your horse.
▸ One or more simple exercises you can use to work on that component.
▸ A checklist so you can assess your progress in a separate journal.
▸ Tips to aid your understanding.

The beauty of this approach is that you can tailor the exercises and your goals to suit your and your horse's experience and skill levels. Every rider who uses this book will approach the training building blocks, the exercises, and the goal-setting processes in a different way.

Let me give you two examples that illustrate the two ends of the equestrian goal-setting spectrum. If a rider were to come to me and say, "I'd like to qualify for the dressage World Cup next year," my response would be, "Okay, your life is going to be a little unbalanced for the next year because you want to do something that's very difficult to attain—only one rider in the country gets to go. Your commitment has to be huge, so not taking the time to train or to work out isn't an option if you want to achieve that goal. You have to be committed to becoming the best you can be. You may have to sacrifice in other areas of your life in the process of trying to make that goal a reality."

On the other end of the spectrum is the person with a lower-level dressage horse, a nine-to-five desk job, a spouse, and children. That person can devote only an hour a day to riding. If he or she were to ask me about a realistic goal, I might respond, "An attainable goal is to ride in your first Training Level class by the end of the season. Let's figure out ways to fit this into your life—to make the most of the time you are able to devote to your riding and your athletic development so that you can reach this goal and feel comfortable and confident."

The working spouse and parent who struggles to fit riding into the schedule has no easier a task than the elite rider who wants to qualify for the World Cup. In fact, in terms of time management and sheer perseverance, the World Cup trainee may well have an easier task than the working parent! So please don't feel discouraged if your goals don't seem as lofty as those of the "star" riders. At the same time, do your best to set yourself up for success by setting realistic and attainable goals. There's nothing wrong with thinking big, but then break that ambitious goal down into doable baby steps. Your will have a checklist of accomplishments in your accompanying notebook. You will feel more confident and encouraged, and so will your horse.

Ready? Let's get started.

2.1
RHYTHM *makes the gaits flow. Here is a young horse moving in good rhythm. I am riding Manhattan.*

CHAPTER TWO

Building Block 1: *Rhythm*

Rhythm (ri th ′əm), n. 1. movement or procedure with uniform or patterned recurrence of a beat, accent, or the like.

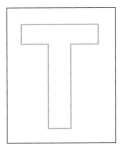

he U.S. Dressage Federation (USDF) defines *rhythm* as "the characteristic sequence of footfalls and phases of a given gait. {For purposes of dressage, the only correct rhythms are those of the pure walk, pure trot, and pure canter (not those of amble, pace, rack, etc.).} Not to be confused with 'tempo' or 'cadence.'"[1]

Many riders confuse rhythm and tempo. Rhythm is the beat of the footfalls (think of the beat of a piece of music you can dance to); tempo is the rate of repetition of those beats within a given period of time. The Germans have a word, takt, which means "the correct tempo for a given gait." A horse moving with takt, then, is neither hurrying nor lazy in his strides but rather is moving at a tempo considered appropriate for the gait and the scope of his stride.

Rhythm is considered the foundation of the training scale because the basis of dressage training is three pure gaits. A walk, trot, or canter that is irregular—that does not maintain a regular rhythm and tempo—is considered a major flaw. To be considered pure, the walk must have a clear four-beat rhythm; the trot, a two-beat rhythm; and the canter, a three-beat rhythm. Loss of rhythm can be caused by loss of balance, lameness and other physical discomfort (ask your veterinarian to rule out physical causes), or even an unbalanced rider. A fluctuating tempo can be caused by inconsistent use of the aids, tension, laziness, or fatigue, to name a few.

Two additional terms that often get thrown in the mix when discussing rhythm are *cadence* and *speed*. The USDF defines *cadence* as a "steady tempo with

1 All USDF definitions in this book are from the *United States Dressage Federation Manual.* U.S. Dressage Federation, 1995.

marked accentuation of the rhythm and beat, with emphasized springiness." Because of the reference to springiness (suspension), the term cadence tends to be used in describing the movement of more advanced dressage horses, who can show more collection and suspension.

Speed is simply velocity, or the rate of travel. Event riders have to concern themselves with speed when they ride cross-country, as the rules dictate that they must travel at a certain number of meters per minute. Speed is not necessarily related to tempo: A horse can take many tiny strides, making for a fast tempo, yet not be moving very quickly across the ground.

RIDER

THE *rhythmic* RIDER

The MIND Element: Tempo and Footfalls

What You Need to Know

The concept of *rhythm*—and its differences from *tempo, speed,* and *cadence*—can be difficult to grasp at first. Remember, rhythm is either regular or irregular; tempo is either fast or slow. Rhythm describes the regularity or evenness of a gait. When we say that a horse is moving in a good rhythm, then, we mean that his footfalls would keep time with a metronome—that he has "a beat you can dance to." Rhythm is what makes the gait flow. A rhythmic horse's limbs are in synch with the rest of his body, and his movement is harmonious and pleasing to watch.

As the rider, you need to develop a keen awareness of rhythm because rhythm relates closely to the *timing* of your aids. When your horse moves in a steady rhythm, you can time your aids exactly, which makes for smoother transitions, more effective half-halts, and prompt flying changes, to name just a few. Good timing requires an acute sensitivity to the feedback you get from your horse. The effectiveness of an aid, an adjustment, or a reaction nearly always depends on its being given at the only instant that it will do any good. Knowing which instant is the right one calls for a combination of intuition and familiarity with your horse, your body, your riding ability, your mental state, and the movement at hand—and that combination adds up to make timing a rather nebulous quality. Some people seem to be born with the gift of timing, but every rider can develop a sense of timing through systematic work.

If you're not sure of how timing works in riding, think about the expert dance partners you may have seen on television, at the ballet, or in a studio or club. Really good dance partners make their partnership look effortless, their movements and strides matched perfectly. There is a flow that captures your attention. But even skilled dancers don't move together fluidly the first time they practice together, even if both partners know the steps. After a while, though, they learn each other's natural movements, reactions, abilities, and responses; and they begin to act without having to test and watch each other as much. Eventually, their communication becomes so subtle that it is invisible to onlookers. It becomes more of a feeling that results from knowing the other's movements so well.

Timing relates to rhythm in the same way that rhythm relates to timing. Just as a good rhythm in your horse's gaits permits you to concentrate on your timing—especially when you're progressing to new areas—accurate timing from you is the only thing that will develop a steady rhythm in a healthy horse.

Assess Your Understanding

Ask yourself the following questions. If you're not sure of an answer, ask your instructor for help.

1. Can you tap your foot in time to a song on the radio and count out the beat?
2. Can you tap your foot and count out the beat in time to a horse's footfalls while watching him in person or on videotape?
3. Can you count out the beat aloud as a horse walks, trots, and canters? For example, a correct canter rhythm sounds like "One-two-three, one-two-three."
4. Can you count out the beat aloud as the horse you're riding walks, trots, and canters?
5. Can you "listen" to the beat silently as you ride? Are you aware of moments when your horse's rhythm becomes irregular?

Were you shaky on any of the items? Which ones? If you identified any weak areas, let's set some goals for improving your understanding of rhythm.

Set Your Goals

In your journal or notebook, write a sentence or two that describes the way that you'd like to improve your understanding and recognition of rhythm, tempo, and footfalls. Keep referring back to your sense of timing and work on achieving a parallel between your horse's rhythm and your timing.

Make this goal—and all the goals you set while using this book—a realistic and achievable step. To help ensure that your goal is realistic, put it to the 30-day test: Is it realistic to expect that I can achieve this goal in 30 days? If the answer is no, break the goal down into smaller steps, and make each small step a 30-day goal. This is the fun part of your training. Write it down when you achieve a goal, and celebrate the reward!

Here are some examples of possible realistic goals regarding rhythm:

"I will learn to keep a beat."

"I will learn to hear and feel my horse's footfalls at the different gaits."

"I will learn to feel the difference between regular and irregular rhythm while I am riding."

Exercise

By this point, intellectually, you should have a good idea of your level of mastery of the concept of rhythm as it relates to tempo and footfalls. Have you identified any areas that need a tune-up? If you have, the following exercise should prove helpful.

Establish a regular working trot on a 20-meter circle. (If your horse is more advanced, establish a collected trot.) As you ride, count the number of strides it takes your horse to make one circle. Make ten circles in each direction and calculate the average number of strides per circle by counting the total number of strides and dividing by 20. The average is your "ballpark" correct rhythm and tempo.

Note: You'll get the best results if you work in a freshly dragged arena. To ensure that your calculation is as accurate as possible, be sure to stay on the exact 20-meter circle you've established.

Next, set a clip-on metronome (available from most music stores) to match the rate you've established, then find music that fits that tempo. The trot is a two-beat gait: "*one-two, one-two*." (My freestyle choreographer, Terri Ciotti Gallo, gives tips on matching music to horses' gaits—see Sidebar, p. 30). Set up a cassette or CD player near the arena so that you'll be able to hear the music while you're riding. Ride the 20-meter circle to the music you've selected until you can maintain a steady tempo and rhythm along with the beat. Next, go down the long side of the arena, change direction, and come back to the 20-meter circle in the other direction. Redo the exercise until you can trot steadily with the beat of the music.

Repeat the entire exercise in the canter (working or collected, depending on your horse's level of training), from establishing your average number of strides per circle to riding to music in both directions while striving to maintain a steady rhythm and tempo. Note that the canter is a three-beat (waltz time) gait: "one-two-*three*, one-two-*three*."

STARTER TUNES

According to well-known freestyle designer and choreographer Terri Ciotti Gallo, whose clients include U.S. Olympic dressage veterans Steffen Peters and Guenter Seidel, "Canters fall in a small tempo range, but trots can go from 138 footfalls per minute (as exhibited by such horses as Graf George, Seidel's 1996 Olympic partner) to 170 footfalls per minute by a smaller, less-collected horse. Ponies can have footfalls up into the 180s. There is no right or wrong. Tempos come in a large range, depending on the size of the horse, impulsion, degree of collection, amount of ground they cover, and so on."

Gallo gave some examples of pieces of music that tend to work well with horses' gaits:

TROT

Quick tempo:

Mambo #5 (Lou Bega)

Moderate tempo:

She Loves You (The Beatles)

In the Mood (Glenn Miller)

Dancing in the Dark (Bruce Springsteen)

Slow tempo:

A Hard Day's Night (The Beatles)

Love Me Do (The Beatles)

The Marriage of Figaro by Mozart: Overture

Other good trot pieces are *Celtic jigs* and *Italian tarantellas.*

CANTER

Rhythm Devine (Enrique Iglesias)

La Isla Bonita (Madonna)

Theme from The Andy Griffith Show

Sergeant Pepper's Lonely Hearts Club Band (The Beatles)

Forever in Blue Jeans (Neil Diamond)

The Impresario by Mozart: Overture

Other good canter pieces are *Joplin rags, Irish reels,* and *sambas.*

WALK

Yellow Submarine (The Beatles)

Visit Terri Ciotti Gallo's website, **www.klassickur.com.** For a few examples of music pieces that are especially suitable to the rhythm and tempo of horses' gaits, see *Starter Tunes* above.

Progress Check

All of the world's top riders and trainers work daily on improving the basics—including their horses' rhythm and tempo. Still, I'm sure you'd like to know how to tell when you've gained sufficient mastery over an element to be able to move on. In the "Progress Check" section of each component, I'll give you a checklist that you can use to gauge your improvement, based on the 30-day goals you've set for yourself.

Here's your checklist for tempo and footfalls.

✔ After 30 days, can you count the footfalls as you watch a horse walk, trot, and canter?

✔ Can you tell whether a horse maintains a steady rhythm and tempo as you watch him go?

✔ Can you count walk, trot, and canter footfalls as you ride?

✔ Can you tell whether the horse you're riding maintains a steady rhythm and tempo?

✔ *Advanced challenge:* Can you tell whether the rhythm and tempo of the horse you're riding are appropriate to his level of development, degree of collection, way of going, and stride length?

The BODY Element: Strength
What You Need to Have

No, you don't have to be Arnold Schwarzenegger to be able to ride competently. You do, however, need a certain amount of basic body strength—the strength to stay aboard a walking, trotting, and cantering horse; to apply seat, leg, and rein aids; to keep your upper body upright in the saddle; and to maintain your form and apply corrections if your horse pulls with his head and neck or makes an unexpected move.

If you lack this basic strength, you'll have difficulty sitting correctly and giving aids that are effective enough to establish and maintain a correct rhythm and tempo. You may feel insecure in the saddle, as if you're being bounced around like a rag doll. And, if your horse spooks or bucks, you may have a difficult time staying on or you may run the risk of falling off entirely. Not only are you unable to use your aids to influence your horse effectively; you also run the risk of injury from stressing weak muscles, not to mention the bumps and bruises you may accumulate if you fall off.

Assess Your Skill Level

Ask your instructor or a knowledgeable helper for input if you're not sure of the answers to the following. Be honest with yourself—and take heart: If you're lacking in any of the following areas, I'll give you exercises that can produce results that you'll notice and appreciate in a relatively short period of time.

Betsy's Tips

Common rhythm and tempo mistakes:

▶ Tempo too fast (horse "chased" forward)

▶ Tempo too slow (horse not active enough)

▶ Tempo not regular and consistent

▶ Tempo "hovers" and is passage-like without being connected from haunches to forehand.

As you work on establishing good rhythm and tempo in your horse's gaits, focus on creating calm and steady steps. Find the correct walk, trot, and canter tempos for your horse, and he'll probably fall naturally into a good rhythm.

1. Can you ride at a trot or canter for 15 minutes or more without becoming winded?
2. Can you sit the trot without feeling as if you're being bounced all over the saddle?
3. Can you walk, trot, and canter without balancing on the reins? (Riders who use the reins for support tend to lean back in a "waterskiing" posture.)
4. If your horse speeds up, slows down, or breaks gait, can you use your position effectively to adjust his gaits?
5. Do you often feel tired, sore, and stiff the day after you ride?

If you answered no to questions 1, 2, 3, or 4 or yes to question 5, you'll benefit from the exercises on page 38.

Set Your Goals

In your journal or notebook, write a sentence or two that describes a goal regarding your overall strength. Be realistic: If you're new to riding or fitness, you're not going to turn into a bodybuilder in a couple of weeks—or even months. Possible realistic goals include:

"I will develop the strength needed to sit the trot without collapsing through my hips and midsection."

"I will strengthen my legs and seat so that I no longer have to lean on the reins for support."

"I will strengthen my arms and upper body so that I can keep my fingers closed on the reins and my shoulders back."

"I will strengthen my legs so that I'm able to use them as strongly (or lightly) as I need to get the desired response from my horse."

Exercise

If you've ever picked up a fitness magazine, you know that there are practically unlimited exercises, programs, and approaches. I've tried many of them, and I've found that the *Pilates* Method is the best all-around way for riders to develop the strength and flexibility that they need for our sport.

Chiropractic physician Dr. Susan Habanova, a certified *Pilates* instructor who provided the *Introduction to Pilates* (see Sidebar on p. 34), worked with me on a sport-specific program for the equestrian athlete. It was decided to combine the two words "equestrian" and "Pilates," so I named the new exercise program *Equilates*. This is the approach to rider athleticism that I will present in this book, and the exercises that appear were selected to address the physical requirements of riding—from "core strength" and flexibility to alignment and total body control—as you and your horse work your way up through the components of the *Classical Training Pyramid*. (To find out more about *Equilates*, or to purchase equipment, log on to www.Equilates.com.)

One of the biggest advantages to using the *Equilates* method is that being a cross-training system, it strengthens and supples the body in much the same way that we want to strengthen and supple our horses' bodies. Most of the exercises that I'll give you in this book can be done in your living room, in a hotel room, or at an athletic-training facility—anywhere you can find or create a comfortable floor surface with some room to move and stretch out. And all you need in the way of attire is comfortable clothing that moves with you and is nonrestrictive. You don't even need shoes; the exercises I'll give you are best done barefoot.

Most of the *Pilates*-based exercises in this book require no equipment other than a mat or a comfortable floor surface. A few exercises call for the use of an exercise ball, a foam roller, or the *Pilates* reformer (the traditional *Pilates* apparatus). You can obtain a ball and a foam roller from most fitness-training facilities, physical therapists, and exercise or yoga catalogs and websites (www.Equilates.com; or www.yogazone.com). You may not have the room or inclination to obtain a reformer for home use, and that's okay; we'll give you mat-based versions of the reformer exercises.

Although you can do the basic *Pilates*-based program at home, I like going into a studio for my sessions. You'll get optimal results by working with a qualified instructor at a *Pilates* studio, where you'll have access to a reformer and other apparatus and will enjoy personalized attention and training. For more information about *Pilates* or to find a *Pilates* studio in your area, visit www.pilates-studio.com.

Of course, these exercises should be done by riders who are in good physical health, and who have consulted a physician before beginning the program. Check with your physician before beginning any type of physical-training program. Should you experience any pain or discomfort during exercise, stop and consult your physician immediately.

INTRODUCTION TO PILATES

By Dr. Susan Habanova,

The Pilates Wellness Center, Wellington, Florida

2.2

Susan Habanova collaborating with Betsy Steiner before a photo shoot.

Pilates (pronounced puh-LAH-teez) is a method of physical and mental conditioning. Its founder, the German-born Joseph H. Pilates (1880-1967), was a frail child who later developed a strengthening and conditioning regimen that he dubbed "contrology"—the complete coordination of body, mind, and spirit.

As a hospital nurse during World War I, Pilates experimented with attaching springs and other equipment to patients' beds to support their ailing limbs while he exercised them. These devices served as the framework for what became the *Pilates* apparatus and the foundation for his style of body conditioning.

After the war, Pilates moved to New York City, where he opened the first *Pilates* Studio® in 1926 and developed a steady following of dancers, performers, and athletes. Today, his methods are enjoying a revival and are used by professional dancers and athletes, by fitness enthusiasts of all persuasions, as well as by orthopedists, chiropractors, and physical therapists.

***Pilates* principles and benefits.** The *Pilates* method stresses form and control over repetitions or duration, with a goal of enhancing awareness of muscle function. This principle produces very positive results when applied to the training of our horses. Most of the exercises target what Joseph Pilates called the "powerhouse"—the abdomen, lower back, and buttocks—the theory being that supporting and strengthening these muscle groups enables the rest of the body to move freely—as do the horse's abdomen, back, and haunches. *Pilates* exercises, which combine stretching and strengthening, facilitate the development of efficient and graceful movement, improved body alignment and breathing, and increased body awareness, just as we want in our horses. The exercises tend to produce leaner, longer muscles than traditional weight training; and they improve balance, coordination, and circulation.

Correct breathing is essential for all sports and forms of exercise, and *Pilates* movements coordinate breathing with the *flow* of an exercise. However, many people find correct breathing quite difficult at first. Once you become more comfortable with the basic *Pilates* concepts, you can concentrate on it more fully, hence its high level in the *Pilates Pyramid* (fig. 2.3).

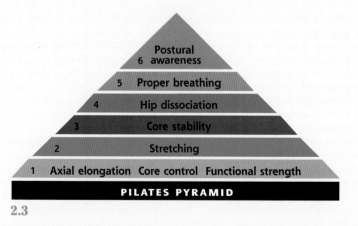

2.3

Pilates work utilizes the following principles and terminology:

The core. There are three abdominal muscles that constitute the core. They are the *transverses abdominis,* the *internal obliques,* and the *external obliques.* The core muscles are *functional* muscles that must be used in a dynamic manner during all movement and in all positions. These core muscles function as a whole and play a pivotal role in body mechanics. The fourth abdominal muscle is the *rectus abdominis.* It is a *structural* muscle, similar to the biceps muscle in your arm, and it responds to isometric contractions. The core muscles need to be engaged, not contracted, therefore the *rectus abdominis* is not part of the core-muscle group (fig. 2.4). (See *Functional vs. Structural Strength* below.)

Axial elongation and *core control:* Axial elongation (lengthening the torso) helps riders to keep a steady, secure seat in the saddle while achieving a tall, elegant look. Axial elongation also promotes proper posture and *engages* the *core,* which enables the rider to have greater functional strength in her arms and legs.

The box. One of the goals of *Pilates* training is *core stability*—a steady, strong torso. *Pilates* defined the torso as "the box", which is a box formed by drawing horizontal lines from shoulder to shoulder and from hip to hip and then by connecting them with two vertical lines drawn from shoulder to hip. The box includes the shoulder girdle, the thoracic and lumbar spine, and the pelvis (fig. 2.5 A). The extremities and the head and neck are therefore "outside the box."

The concept of the box can also be applied to the horse. The horse's box would be formed by drawing horizontal lines from shoulder to haunches on both sides and then by drawing vertical lines from shoulder to shoulder and from haunches to haunches. Because of the horse's larger and longer neck, more of his body than yours falls outside the box (fig. 2.5 B).

Functional vs. structural strength. *Structural muscles* are muscles that can be contracted (e.g., the biceps and inner thighs). Structural strength refers to how strong these muscles are on their own, (e.g., how many pounds you can lift in a biceps curl). *Functional* muscles are used in conjunction with structural muscles to enhance structural muscles' performance. Functional muscles stabilize certain body parts, thereby freeing up the structural muscle to "focus" on the effort. *Pilates* instructors refer to the concept of "central stability for distal mobility": If your core is stabilized, your distal parts (those outside the box) can be more mobile. Using the example of the biceps curl, the exercise will feel easier—and you may be able to curl more weight—if you *engage your core* and *stabilize your box.*

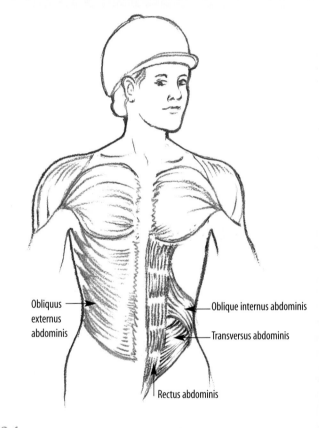

Obliquus externus abdominis

Oblique internus abdominis

Transversus abdominis

Rectus abdominis

2.4

The transverses abdominis, and internal and external obliquus are the deep underlying muscles that make up your "core."

Riding requires a great deal of biomechanical stability in your shoulder girdle and pelvis. If either is not stabilized to the spine, then you will have trouble controlling your arms and legs. Your functional muscular strength will be diminished, and you will be forced to compensate by shifting your body weight, which will affect your horse's balance. The stronger your functional muscles and the more centered your core, the more centered you can keep your horse.

The importance of stretching. Learning how to isolate and use muscles with which you are not familiar can be difficult. Doing so can be even more challenging if you are unable to get to the muscles in the first place. For example, most people have a bit of undesirable subcutaneous tissue (fat) in the low abdominal area—which gives rise to the common complaint that abdominal exercises are ineffective. The reason for this is the lack of movement in the lower back. The *transverse abdominis* core muscle wraps around the waist and attaches to the deepest muscle layers in the lower back. If the lower-back vertebrae do not move independently then the corresponding abdominal muscles cannot be used or strengthened. If you can start to separate movement in your lower back, your abdominals will respond. This fine control over movement is key in terms of stability and mobility in riding.

Stillness in motion. *Core stability and shock absorption:* When you ride, your horse transmits movement from the ground up and into your lower extremities. Without core stability, the movement will travel all the way up into your shoulders, neck, and head. With core stability, you can absorb the shock in your lower body without collapsing, twisting, bouncing, or bobbing your upper body. The principle also works in reverse: You can use core stability to influence your horse, and you can selectively utilize the transmission of energy from your lower body into your spine, such as when you are asking your horse for improved contact or impulsion (more on contact and impulsion in Chapters Four and Five).

Proper breathing. Learning how to organize your trunk through breathing can help you in understanding and developing core stability. Using the core muscles to facilitate breathing

A

2.5 A & B
The rider's "box". Use of your core muscles enables you to find your stability **(A)**.

Likewise, the horse's stability is found within his own box **(B)**.

B

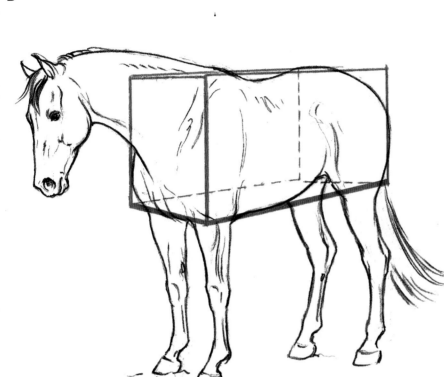

relaxes many of the upper-body and shoulder muscles, which, in turn, enables the shoulders, head, neck, and wrists to be more relaxed.

Postural awareness. To achieve proper upper-body posture, the upper spine must be able to flatten instead of rounding, the shoulder blades must be held toward each other, and the muscles at the front of the neck must be strong enough to hold the head over the shoulders. *Pilates* exercises are designed to produce this proper posture.

How does Pilates apply to riding? Classical *Pilates* movements were performed with a flat back (a posterior pelvic tilt), which is similar to a rider's body position. Newer *Pilates*-based programs call for a *neutral spinal and pelvic position,* which more closely resembles everyday movement. A flat back or *posterior pelvic tilt* causes the *core* abdominal muscles to disengage. Therefore, it is advised that the *Pilates* exercises be performed first with a *neutral* pelvis to establish proper *core control* or engagement, and then with a *posterior pelvic tilt* after your *Pilates* foundation is in place.

Although *Pilates* is my choice for all-around strength and suppleness training for the rider, there may be times when you find you need other types of exercise—aerobic workouts, weight training, t'ai chi, or others. I recognize the value of these programs and use them myself in my own athletic-training regimen. However, to maintain the continuity of the exercises in this book, you will find Equilates a well-rounded training method that will help you achieve better results in your riding.

The rider exercises in this book are structured so that, just as in the *Classical Training Pyramid* for your horse, one concept builds on another. My goal is to train horse and rider in the same manner: by maintaining and applying layer of learning as you begin working on the next. Develop a foundation, take it with you; add a layer to the foundation, take it with you.

EXERCISE: Axial Elongation to Promote Functional Strength

As you've learned, the *Pilates* method focuses on the development of a core stability (see Sidebar, p. 34). In the exercises, as well as when you're in the saddle, your core functional abdominal muscles need to be engaged, not contracted. The key to accomplishing this is axial elongation (lengthening of the torso), which creates a leaner, longer, firmer silhouette and helps your body to become functionally strong. By achieving this, you'll be better able to control your body movements and to give more precise aids to your horse. As a rider, you need to be able to sit tall and to feel your horse's strides. The exercise that follows will help your body to become a conduit to feel his tempo and rhythm (fig. 2.6).

Stand with your feet shoulder-width apart. Inhale and imagine that a string is attached to the top of your head. Then, as you exhale, imagine the string pulling you upward, drawing energy from your pelvic floor up toward the crown of your head. As you do so, visualize the string drawing you tall and erect; you may even "grow" about one-quarter of an inch during this exercise. Lengthen your midsection between your ribs and hips (this draws in your core), and funnel your lower ribs to your hips without collapsing the upper body. Allow your sternum (breastbone) to lift as you slide your shoulder blades down into your back pockets (fig. 2.7).

This exercise may seem difficult at first, but with practice, it should become very easy. Start in the standing position; next, try it in the saddle at the halt. After you feel as if you have the hang of it, try it while you walk and ride in all three gaits.

At first, you will need to concentrate on maintaining this new body position, but after a little practice axial elongation will feel more natural. You may even feel

2.6

My Pilates instructor, Dr. Susan Habanova, demonstrates a posture that's not axially elongated. Her shoulders are forward, her neck is out, her abdominal muscles are not engaged, and she's stressing her lower back. A horse could easily pull a rider with this posture forward and off balance.

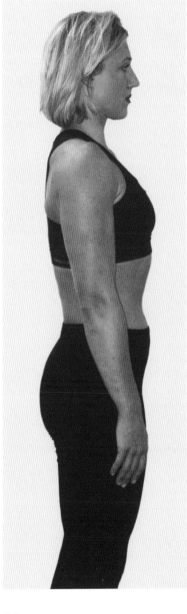

as if you're not standing erect when you're not doing it. At this point, axial elongation will have become a habit and will require less conscious effort. You'll begin to integrate it into your everyday activities and movements.

Progress Check

With this and all of the *Pilates* exercises to follow, compare your progress in the exercises with your progress in the saddle. Are you finding that your riding improves as you master the exercises?

For this section, use the checklist below to gauge your improvement. When you can answer yes to the following questions (get a second opinion from your instructor or a knowledgeable helper if you're not sure), you're ready to move on.

2.7

What a difference axial elongation makes! Here Susan's abs are engaged, her posture is erect and aligned, and her lower back is protected. (She also looks thinner, and more elegant!)

✔ Do you feel secure as you sit the trot and canter?

✔ Does your seat remain still yet is able to follow your horse's movement?

✔ Can you extend first one, and then both hands forward as you ride without losing your balance or your position in the saddle?

✔ Can you drop your stirrups for a few strides and maintain your balance and position?

✔ If your horse doesn't respond to a light leg aid, can you give him a stronger squeeze and get a response?

✔ If your horse "roots" or pulls on the reins, can you close your fingers on the reins and tighten the muscles in your arms (without pulling backward) to resist him until he softens?

✔ Can you keep your body aligned in all three gaits, with your ears, shoulder, hips, and heels all in a line?

The SPIRIT Element: Patience
What You Need to Be

The foundation of *gymnastic training* is repetition—of aids, of corrections, of exercises. Horses learn through many, many repetitions. In her book *Dressage with Kyra*, renowned Finnish dressage trainer, competitor, and clinician Kyra Kyrklund writes that it takes up to 100,000 repetitions to make a new pattern a reflex. To do anything 100,000 times consistently, correctly, and without becoming frustrated or irritated takes patience. Patience is the ability to keep coming back and giving additional explanations to the horse until he understands. First, patience requires faith that what you're doing is right. Then you must develop self-discipline and emotional control, which will guide you in knowing when to praise your horse and when to correct him. Disciplining—correcting—is actually an important component of patience. If you're a parent or ever have spent time around children, you know that it's easier to say yes than to say no! To say no when you know the child will whine or complain—and to continue saying no in the face of badgering—takes patience. It's the same when working with horses.

Patience is the willingness to try again and again, while maintaining a positive attitude. The positive attitude is the difference between true patience and stubbornness. When faced with an ongoing problem or resistance, a patient rider explores the reasons for her horse's reluctance or inability to comply and looks for another option. The stubborn person asks the horse in the same way over and over, becomes frustrated, and eventually becomes impatient with both herself and her horse. Patience will always guide you to your goals more quickly than will impatience or stubbornness. If you are patient, you will begin to think of mistakes as opportunities and to become more creative in finding solutions. By using this approach, you won't waste time on ineffective techniques or unfairness toward your horse, and you'll find the method that works best for him and you more quickly. You will learn from what doesn't work as well as from what does.

It also takes patience to work on yourself. We all have position flaws or bad habits that are so ingrained that they feel "right," or occur without conscious thought. It's tremendously difficult to change your body or a pattern of behavior because the new posture or reaction requires so much work to retrain your muscles and your mind-to-body reactions. When you're trying to change yourself, you need to be patient with yourself—to allow yourself the time (and the many repetitions that it will require for the new behavior to become habit) that you need without giving up or succumbing to negative self-talk ("I'm so out of shape, I'll never be able to sit the trot"; "I just don't get it, and I'll never learn how to do a shoulder-in").

Patience is also empathy for the demands you're placing on your horse. If you lift weights in the gym, you know how difficult it is to do that last repetition when your muscles are burning and all you want to do is stop. If you jog or ride a bike or work out on a Stairmaster, you know how hard the last minute can be. Your understanding can help give you patience when it comes to your horse; you'll know how he's feeling when he's tired and you're asking for that little bit more. You'll know that, just as a body builder needs to rest between sets, giving your horse short breaks during his workouts actually can improve his performance.

Assess Your Psyche

It's human nature to be able to assess other people's personalities, strengths, and weaknesses easily yet have difficulty doing the same with ourselves. When it comes to ourselves, many of us tend to be either overcritical or a little blind to our quirks and foibles. As a result, some of you may find the psychological self-assessments more difficult than their intellectual and physical counterparts. Be honest with yourself. Identify aspects of your nature that you'd like to work on or change, and accept doing so as fun and a challenge. After all, none of us is perfect, there is

Betsy's Tips

Patience is not passive—it does not imply that you accept whatever naughtiness your horse cares to dish out. Rather, patience means asking and asking again with the desired amount of firmness you wish to have, but all the while remaining emotionally impassive. If you're patient, you're not attached to or wrapped up in the outcome because you know that it doesn't reflect on you personally; you're simply training and learning from each other. You have faith that what you're doing will eventually bring the desired result. You're not worried about looking incompetent or foolish or ineffective; you're willing to continue asking until your horse figures it out.

Patience also means not being reactive. If you're asking your horse to make a 20-meter circle at B, say, and every time he reaches B he spooks at the letter, falls out of rhythm, and stops focusing on his work, you don't get all caught up in the spook, overreacting to the fact that he's not paying attention. Instead, you may choose either to continue to give the aids in the same way, making corrections as needed and not tensing with anticipation of the spook; or to patiently move on to some other work so as to change the situation.

always something that we can work on. The goal of these psychological sections is to help you identify, understand, and develop those characteristics that can deepen your relationship with your horse, help you get more enjoyment out of your riding, and improve your skill as an athlete. You'll probably get to know yourself better along the way. And who knows? You may happen on some insights that resonate in other areas of your life—that's part of the power and the gift of the relationship you can develop with your horse through riding.

Read the following statements. Identifying with more than one indicates that patience may not be your strong suit.

1. After a difficult schooling session, I tend to feel "down" for the remainder of the day.
2. I'm finding it difficult to squelch negative self-talk during and after a bad ride.
3. I love my horse, but sometimes I lose my temper with him when he acts resistant.
4. I get frustrated easily while I'm riding.
5. Things like getting stuck in traffic, having to wait in line, and getting put on hold upset me and affect the way that I later react to my horse—and to people.

Set Your Goals

In your journal or notebook, write a sentence or two that describes a realistic goal regarding patience. Be specific. Examples:

"I will stop, take a deep breath, and count to ten if I feel myself losing my temper with my horse. I'll go through my mental checklist and ask myself what I may have done to cause his behavior."

"If the approach I'm using isn't producing results after three sessions, I will regroup and think of another way to try to explain to my horse what I want."

"If I try everything I can think of and still am having trouble with a concept or movement, I will seek the advice of a professional trainer."

"I'm going to change the way I think about 'mistakes' and choose instead to see them as opportunities."

Exercises

This may surprise you, but I'm going to give you a physical exercise in this section to help you practice patience. I'm betting that, as you work to improve your strength and fitness, you'll gain empathy for your horse. You'll also learn about the patience and perseverance needed to reach even a modest goal.

Establish a working or collected walk on a 20-meter circle. Begin counting aloud along with your horse's tempo: "One, two, three, four…." Strive to keep both the tempo and your counting very methodical and consistent. Don't allow him to wander off the line of your circle. Monitor your internal self-talk and replace any negative words or thoughts with statements of opportunity. Above all, practice using patience. Next, try this exercise in the trot and the canter and in the opposite direction.

As you circle, remind yourself to use your *core stability*. Be patient with yourself. Work to develop a sense of emotional detachment. Imagine that you are an instructor, watching yourself ride. Of course, you want to see progress and improvement, but you're not upset or critical if everything isn't perfect. Be analytical rather than emotional: Steadily and continuously work your core stability—you'll develop patience and great abs at the same time!

Progress Check

It's difficult to measure patience, which is a quality and therefore is hard to quantify. I think you'll know when you're riding and training with more patience. If you ask yourself the following questions, your "patience quotient" should become fairly apparent.

✔ Do I remain emotionally nonreactive when I'm riding, even if my horse seems to misbehave intentionally?

✔ Am I willing to repeat tomorrow what I did today, and the next day, and the day after that, until my horse catches on?

✔ If I discipline or correct my horse, do I do so fairly and then "let go" of the incident?

✔ Do I feel inspired about the way I worked with my horse today, even if I only took a small step forward?

HORSE

THE *rhythmic* HORSE

The MIND Element: Leg Equals "Forward"

What Your Horse Needs to Know

It's easy to sum up what the horse needs to understand at this most elementary level of training. Leg comes on: I go forward. That's really all there is to it. His response should be in a forward motion; he is not to lean against the leg kick out at it, or ignore it. The forward response is the foundation of training because there can be no rhythm, suppleness, contact, impulsion, straightness, or collection if there is no willing forward motion.

When you consider how fundamental the forward response is to *gymnastic training*, it may come as something of a surprise to realize that many of the horses in clinics and at shows appear never to have been taught this concept thoroughly. Some horses "hold back" against the leg; they are not truly in front of the leg. Some show their lack of acceptance by delaying their reaction or by kicking out at the leg, the whip, or the spur. Others react to the leg by leaning against it instead of moving away. Most horses are inclined toward one or more of these reactions, and so reinforcing and honing the desired forward response remains an important part of schooling throughout a horse's career, even at the highest levels.

Of course, even the best trained, most obedient horse can be made dull or insensitive to the leg if his rider does not have enough strength and control to keep her legs from bouncing against his sides. After a while, the feeling of her heels against his sides becomes a sort of kinesthetic "white noise": He simply tunes out the irritation. And a horse that's been abused with a whip may be whip-shy yet not truly "hot" in his reaction to the whip or to the leg. Such a horse may or may not be able to be retrained to accept his rider carrying and using a whip without panicking; but his issue is one of trust, not of an understanding of going forward.

Assess Your Horse's Understanding

Use the following checklist to evaluate your horse's understanding and acceptance of the leg-equals-forward concept.

1. Does your horse move forward promptly from a light squeezing of your lower legs against his sides?

2. Do you frequently have to give leg aids more than once, or with increasing insistence, before he responds?

3. Does he tend to kick out or wring his tail irritably instead of going forward when you use your leg or touch him with the spur or the whip?

4. When you apply a leg aid, do you feel as if your horse "sucks back" instead of stepping forward?

5. When you apply a leg aid, does your horse tighten the muscles along his sides and "push back" against you instead of feeling as if he softens through his ribs and steps forward?

If you answered no to question 1 and yes to at least one of questions 2 through 5, your horse needs a refresher course in "forward from the leg."

Set Your Goals

In your journal or notebook, write a sentence or two that describes a realistic goal for increasing your horse's understanding and acceptance of the leg aid. Examples:

"I will accept only a response to a light leg aid. If my horse does not respond, I will check my position and my way of asking him to go forward. When I'm sure that I am asking correctly, I will repeat the light leg aid to test his obedience. If he does not respond, I will repeat the sequence until he responds promptly to a light aid."

"I will teach my horse that kicking out at my leg is not acceptable."

Exercises

Each of the following exercises is designed to help your horse learn to understand and accept your leg aids.

EXERCISE 1: Yielding to the Leg

Establish a calm and regular working (or collected, if your horse is more advanced) walk on a 20-meter circle. As you walk away from the rail, ask him to take one step sideways, away from your inside leg. Immediately take a step forward, and then ask for one or two steps of turn on the forehand, maintaining contact with your out-

2.8 A – C Leg-Yield to Turn on the Forehand

As I begin, I ask Manhattan to flex to the inside as I push his haunches over to the left with my right leg (A).

As he takes a step sideways in the leg-yield, I prevent his shoulders from falling to the left by closing my upper left leg and driving with my seat, which supports the contact into the left rein (B).

side rein to prevent him from stepping forward. Walk forward several strides and repeat the exercise. Do the exercise in both directions until your horse steps away from your leg promptly and obediently (figs. 2.8 A – C).

If your horse does not move away from your inner leg correctly, use reinforcing aids to help him get the idea and learn that he must yield to your inner leg by stepping forward and sideways with his inner hind leg. If you get no response to

C

The right hind leg crosses well underneath his body as Manhattan begins the turn on the forehand **(C)**.

Rider's Tip: *Remember to engage your core and keep the horse forward.*

your initial seat and lower-leg aids, reinforce the aid by using your lower leg alone against his side. If your lower leg gets no response, give him a little kick with your spur. Use the spur and then relax your leg; don't dig the spur into his side and hold it there. If the spur fails to produce an acceptable response, tap him once directly behind your leg with your whip (2.9 A – C).

A

B

I begin use of the spur against the horse's side. (As you begin to apply the spur, you may find that your heel rises slightly) **(B).**

C

I demonstrate added support through use of the whip behind my leg **(C).**

2.9 A – C

Correct Leg Positions

I am showing a correct lower leg lying against the horse's side **(A).**

Rider's Tip: *Remember to keep your upper leg closed against the horse from hip to knee when you use your lower leg.*

EXERCISE 2: Leg-Yielding on a Circle

Establish a steady and relaxed working (or collected) walk on a 20-meter circle. Keeping your horse's forehand on the arc of the circle, flex his nose slightly to the inside with your inside rein and push his haunches to the outside for a stride or two with your seat and inner leg. As soon as he softens and yields, relax your inner leg and return to normal bend on the circle. Repeat in both directions. When he is yielding his haunches easily and quietly in the walk, pick up a working (or collected) trot and repeat the exercise (figs 2.10 A – C).

A | B | C

Progress Check

You'll probably have a pretty good idea as to whether your horse's understanding and acceptance of the leg is improving, but here are some benchmarks to consider:

✔ Does my horse now respond to a light leg aid at least 90 percent of the time?

✔ If my horse's tendency is to kick out at the leg or the whip, can I now use those aids and get an obedient response at least 90 percent of the time?

✔ Does my horse feel as if he yields through his rib cage and moves forward with a surge of energy when I apply a leg aid?

2.10 A — C Leg-Yield on a Circle
*Jessie begins in walk with slight flexion to the inside as she moves Magdalena into leg-yield at the trot **(A)**. Notice how Maggie bends around Jessie's right leg as Jessie pushes her to the left, and Maggie crosses over with her inside front leg **(B)**. The leg-yield continues with the inside hind leg crossing to the left **(C)**.*

Rider's Tip: *Engage your core and use your obliques in a sideways motion.*

Betsy's Tips

A correct forward response to leg aids is essential to establishing a correct rhythm and tempo. A horse that "sucks back" behind the leg, leans against the leg, or generally is lazy to the leg, doesn't build up enough forward momentum for a solid rhythm and tempo to emerge. Likewise, a horse that reacts to the leg by kicking out has effectively trained his rider not to touch his sides with her legs. He's got her between the proverbial rock and a hard place: She now has no base of support, and she also can't establish and maintain the forward rhythm that's so important in gymnastic training.

When you ride, think of creating energy and quick responses by using less rather than more. Remember to reward your horse when he responds correctly by giving him a pat on the neck, by softening your rein, or by praising him with your voice. And always be patient: Give him the time he needs to understand and react.

The BODY Element: Strength
What Your Horse Needs to Have

You may have noticed that the *body* element for the horse at this stage of training is the same as it is for the rider. Your horse needs to have a certain amount of basic strength in the muscles of his abdomen, hindquarters, shoulders, and base of his neck to support his back, which is the connector (his "core" or center) between his haunches and his forehand. That basic strength also enables him to carry a rider; to balance himself; and to start, stop, and turn in all three gaits.

Assess Your Horse's Skill Level

If your horse possesses sufficient basic strength, he should be able to do the following:

1. Walk, trot, and canter (with walk breaks) for a 30- to 45-minute schooling session without become unduly fatigued or overheated.
2. Maintain a basic level of organization throughout his body while changing gaits or tempo with sufficient strength to support his own body and his rider's.

Set Your Goals

In your journal or notebook, write a sentence or two that describes a realistic goal for improving your horse's basic strength. Examples:

"I will condition my horse so that he's able to reasonably balance himself through corners, execute 20-meter circles, and make transitions among all three gaits while maintaining his rhythm and balance."

"I will strengthen my horse's hindquarter, abdominal, and back muscles so that he can do transitions without hollowing his back or raising his head and neck for balance."

Exercise

The following exercise is excellent for improving your horse's overall strength and is especially good for his hindquarter, back, and abdominal muscles.

EXERCISE: Hill Work

If you have access to a moderate hill or two (a gently rolling hill, not a steep slope), you have a ready-made piece of "exercise equipment" that's terrific for strengthening your horse's entire body, and particularly his hindquarters, back, and abdominal muscles. (Before you begin hill work, make sure that the ground is relatively even and free of holes. Use common sense by doing hill work only when the footing is good—don't go out when it's muddy or slick, or if it presents any other safety hazards to your horse.)

Start by walking up and down the hill once or twice. Use a "slalom" (serpentine) approach going up and coming down to lessen the strain on the joints of your horse's legs. Keep your upper body positioned over his center of gravity by assuming a modified two-point position (weight in your heels, seat slightly out of the saddle, upper body inclined slightly forward, hands "giving" forward to allow your horse to use his head and neck freely), and ask him to stride evenly up the hill in a serpentine from base to crest. Descend the hill by keeping your upper body very tall and on or slightly behind the vertical, your heels at or slightly in front of the girth for stability, and your horse "hugged" between your legs and your hands for support. Maintain a steady, even pace on the ascent and descent—no lunging forward or gathering speed like a rolling stone. Remember, don't come straight down the hill; use the slalom method, making equal numbers of left and right curves.

Negotiate your hill two or three times a week until your horse strides comfortably and without becoming winded. At that point, try trotting up the hill and walking down your slalom line; you can trot down the same line if the slope is very gentle, but don't go straight down the hill. Trotting downhill at a steep angle places too much stress on the joints and soft tissues.

Before you begin a program of hill work, be sure that your horse is on a good nutritional program (check with your veterinarian if you're not sure) and that he's getting enough of the right things to eat. Keep in mind that you may need to adjust his feeding program as you increase his work and level of conditioning. Your veterinarian can advise you as to the safest and best way to adjust your horse's feed regimen if needed.

Betsy's Tips

Allow for a rest period—even if it's just a minute or two in walk—during any strength-training session so that you don't overstress your horse's muscles. Don't work him to the point of exhaustion, but do enough work to help him build muscle. It's okay if he seems a little tired after a session, but he shouldn't be dragging with fatigue. Stop before he's completely out of gas.

After each workout, take note of where your horse sweats. You'll be able to see which muscles he's used through his sweat patterns.

Progress Check

You'll know your horse has gained sufficient basic strength when he's able to do the following:

✔ Go through a training session (with sufficient walk breaks) and still have energy at the end.

✔ Shows that he's filled out, with increased muscle mass and roundness, at the end of 30 days of strength training. Take photographs or a video of your horse from the front and from the side before you start the program. After a month of training, take another set of photos or video from the same angles.

The SPIRIT Element: Obedience and Work Ethic

What Your Horse Needs to Be

Just like young children, young horses have to learn that there are times when it's okay to play, and there are times when they have to pay attention and do what's asked of them. It's asking a lot of an active six-year-old child to sit still and concentrate for ten minutes. Likewise, it's asking a lot of a playful four- or five-year-old horse to ignore his buddies frolicking out in the field and dutifully walk, trot, and canter for half an hour. In his initial training, the young horse has to be taught to wait for his rider's command before he acts; he has to learn that he can't just do whatever he feels like doing. That's obedience.

A work ethic goes hand in hand with obedience, but they're not the same thing. A horse with a solid work ethic focuses his energies on doing what his rider asks, not on resisting or evading. This type of horse *likes* to work. This is not to say that all resistance or evasion is a sign of a diminished work ethic; even the most hard-working horse may simply be fresh and enthusiastic, may not understand your directions, or may be tired or muscle-sore from yesterday's workout. In general, though, the horse with a strong work ethic spends more time and energy actually working and trying to please his rider than on finding ways to get out of work!

These psychological components in the horse, like the others I'll address in the chapters to come, have a sort of "nature versus nurture" element to them. Like humans, horses are born with distinct personalities, likes, and dislikes. Their personalities, as ours, are shaped by their experience and environment; still, they show certain core characteristics and traits. In the field of human psychology, researchers have begun to realize that genetics play a bigger role in personality than once was thought. Studies of identical twins who were separated at birth, for example, have shown that most twins have remarkably similar personalities and tastes, even if they were reared in very different circumstances. Equine genetics play the same role. A horse that is essentially timid, for instance, probably cannot be transformed through handling or training into a fearless individual, although you may be able to teach him to be less timid. And a horse that would really rather be grazing out in the field and hanging with his buddies than jumping fences may learn that he has to work, but he probably won't become an equine superstar performer.

Because of the inherent nature of horses' psychological qualities, it's important to try to choose a horse whose personality and characteristics mesh with the job that you have in mind for him. But even if you find that your horse lacks a little in the work-ethic department, there are things that you can do to develop that quality.

Set Your Goals

In your journal or notebook, write a sentence or two describing (1) your horse's current level of obedience and work ethic, and (2) a realistic goal regarding those qualities. Consider his basic nature, the job you want him to do, and his attitude toward work. Examples:

"My horse only concentrates for a few minutes at a time. He is easily distracted and doesn't pay attention to my aids."

"I will devise a systematic schooling plan to help keep my horse's interest in and attention on his work so that he focuses on me and the task at hand during our training sessions."

"I will reinforce my horse's positive reactions with praise to help make schooling sessions more enjoyable and rewarding for him."

"I will try always to set my horse up for success by making fair and reasonable demands of him."

Exercises

The following exercises can help reinforce or develop your horse's obedience and work ethic.

2.11

In a perfect halt you will see two legs only from the side view. In training, if your horse is not quite perfect, like this halt, accept the good qualities of obedience and attentive behavior. Although Manhattan is not perfectly square, I would accept this halt because he is nearly square and maintains all the positive qualities of forward energy, even balance, and alertness to my aids.

EXERCISE 1: Obedience Tune-Up

Practice walk-halt transitions. This may sound simple, but done correctly, they are good tests of your horse's obedience. The keys are:

▶ A *precise* (but not hurried or tense) move-off into the walk.

▶ Maintenance of a *steady* walk rhythm and tempo.

▶ A *prompt* (but not abrupt) transition to the halt.

▶ *Immobility* in the halt (no fussing, fidgeting, or looking around) until you give the aids to walk.

▶ *Attention* on you at all times.

Do lots of walk-halt transitions, and you'll help to give your horse the idea that he has to pay attention to you and that, while you're in charge, he must do as you ask. When he's good, let him know it (fig. 2.11).

EXERCISE 2: Positive Reinforcement

If someone praises your efforts—on the job, during a riding lesson, or at home— you feel good about yourself and may even try harder, right? Well, your horse responds to praise in much the same way. This "exercise" is not only a gymnastic movement, but it also provides a definite line of communication to your horse.

To encourage your horse to maintain (or develop) a good work ethic, be sure to reward him when he makes a good effort to please you. Don't just reward a correctly executed movement; reward him when he tries, even if he makes a mistake or doesn't do everything perfectly. Be sympathetic toward him.

Riders need to be aware that positive reinforcement (praise) comes in a variety of actions and degrees. Giving the rein and relaxing your seat and legs after a half-halt is a form of reward, but this "giving" does not carry the same weight as a bona fide reward. So when he makes a good effort, pat him on the neck and praise him with your voice. If it's an appropriate time, you can let him walk on a loose rein. You can also use your voice to encourage him as you're riding—but be aware that using your voice is prohibited in some competitions (figs. 2.12 A & B).

Progress Check

The progress checks for this and the other *spirit* elements are not checklists like the other progress checks in this book. Instead, they are more like opportunities for quiet reflection—about why your horse does what he does, his aptitudes and attitudes, your relationship with him, your riding goals, your compatibility as partners, and ultimately his suitability for the job you've chosen for him.

Take some time to think about the following questions. You may find it helpful to discuss them with someone who knows you and your horse well, such as your instructor. As you ponder the questions, think about things that your instructor or other knowledgeable people may have said to you about your horse. Do any of the issues sound familiar, as if you've heard them before but perhaps didn't really acknowledge them or admit that they might be valid concerns?

2.12

Jessie rewards Magdalena during the workout by giving her the inside rein and patting the mare's neck **(A).**

And, after the session, by patting the mare and letting her walk on a loose rein **(B).**

In order for this kind of evaluation to be productive, you must be honest with yourself about your horse's strengths and weaknesses; and your likes, dislikes, skill level, and riding goals. It can be difficult not to let our own egos or stubbornness get in the way, or to recognize that our goals have changed, or to admit that we're not experienced enough (or brave enough) to handle a particular horse safely and confidently. I see many mismatched horses and riders as a result of such obstacles. Realize that, by being honest with yourself, you're doing both yourself and your horse a favor. There is nothing wrong with making a change if it's in your and his best interests. You're thinking about what's best for you and for him, and you're considering him as a thinking, feeling member of the partnership. In short, you're being a true horseman. Now for the questions:

- ✔ Is basic obedience a constant issue in my training? Do I find myself continually referring to "trying to *make* him do such-and-such" or "having trouble getting him to do anything I want"?

- ✔ If my horse is frequently disobedient, do I understand why? Have I done what I can to eradicate the cause? If there appears to be no legitimate reason for him to resist, does he continue doing so?

- ✔ Is his overall demeanor happy to see me and to go out and work, or does he act sullen and resistant when I greet him, groom him, tack him up, and ride?

- ✔ Do I look forward to my riding sessions, or do they feel like a chore?

- ✔ Is my horse happy and contented as long as he's not being asked to work?

Betsy's Tips

Get in the habit of monitoring your horse's health and well-being daily. Spend unmounted time with him, and learn what's normal—his waking, resting, eating, drinking, eliminating, and behavior patterns. Make him as comfortable as possible, whether it's ensuring a clean and well-bedded stall, blanketing and unblanketing him as needed in chilly weather, installing fans or erecting a run-in shed to help him deal with summer's heat, keeping pests at bay with fly spray and fly masks, or making sure that his tack and equipment fit comfortably.

I'll always advise you to seek input from your instructor or another reputable professional when it comes to problems with your horse, but you also have to learn to trust your own training and your instincts. You know your horse better than anyone else; allow him to be your teacher, too. Ask yourself: Is he happy with his career and his lot in life? Does he like what he's doing? If you could do it all over again, would you choose this horse again to be your partner? If it were up to him, do you think that he would choose you?

3.1
SUPPLENESS: *The horse requires relaxed, harmonious interaction of every joint and muscle.*

CHAPTER THREE

Building Block 2: *Suppleness*

Suppleness (sup′əl•ness), *n.*
1. ability to bend easily without damage; pliant; flexible. 2. characterized by ease in bending; limber; lithe.

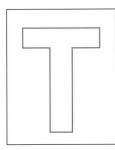

T he USDF defines *suppleness* as a combination of lateral (side-to-side) flexibility, and longitudinal (front-to-back) balance. The *USDF Manual* contains an excerpt from the *British Horse Society (BHS) Manual of Equitation* that offers an excellent explanation of the concept of suppleness:

> *The aim is a suppleness which allows the relaxed co-ordination of every muscle and joint. Tension is the major restriction on such an aim....The most common area of tension is the back—for the horse naturally tends to stiffen and become rigid under the weight of the rider....*
>
> *To supple him laterally he must learn to bend round the rider's inside leg....He must not be allowed to increase the weight on the inside rein and must be encouraged to engage the inside hind leg....*
>
> *To supple him longitudinally means that:*
> - *He brings his hind legs more underneath his body.*
> - *He learns to lift and swing his back.*
> - *He makes his top line rounder by lengthening the muscles along his back and neck.*[1]

In the German training system, the suppleness concept is called *losgelassenheit*. In his book *The Dressage Horse*, former German national dressage coach Harry Boldt explains, "When the horse goes rhythmically, and the rider is able to

---

1 *USDF Manual,* p. 209. BHS excerpt reprinted with permission of Half Halt Press.

push, the horse relaxes his neck and back muscles, obtaining a deeper neck flexion, thus enabling the quarters to be drawn under his body. This achieved, the horse is losgelassen."[2] Boldt goes on to explain that the so-called "stretching circle," in which the rider allows the horse to gradually take the reins out of the hands while stretching forward and down, is a good test of *losgelassenheit*. (USA Equestrian—formerly known as the American Horse Shows Assocation—added the "stretching circle" to the Training and First Level dressage tests in 1999.)

As the USDF and the BHS explain, *gymnastic training* aims to produce two kinds of suppleness: *lateral* and *longitudinal*. A horse that is supple *laterally* is able to step sideways, to bend through his midsection, and to "swing" his back as he moves. A horse that is supple *longitudinally* can stretch down with his neck to seek contact with the bit, step well under his body with his hind legs, reach freely forward with his forelegs from the shoulder, and lift his back.

Smoothness of movement is the manifestation of suppleness. When your horse is able to reposition the muscles in his body and to lengthen and shorten his stride smoothly and without stiffness, he is supple.

---

2 *USDF Manual,* p. 160. Excerpt reprinted with permission of Edition Haberbeck.

RIDER
THE *supple* RIDER

The MIND Element: Purpose of the Aids

What You Need to Know

Much has been written about the aids—traditionally, the rider's seat, legs, and hands—and how to apply them in order to produce the various movements and transitions between gaits. Simply put, the aids are your primary means of communication with your horse. They're the media you use to ask him to flex, bend, turn, and use himself in ways that will make him more supple and elastic. Before you can use your body to apply those aids to supple your horse, you have to understand what the aids are and how they affect the horse (fig. 3.2). (Of course, your body must be supple before you can expect your horse's body to be supple; more about your own suppleness on p. 66.) As a rider, you use different parts of your body to help your horse to balance his body. If you don't understand how the parts of your body influence your horse's body, you'll find it impossible to apply the aids correctly and effectively.

Given correctly, every aid begins with your *seat*, which includes your abdominal, lower-back, and gluteal muscles, and your upper legs. Think of your seat as the trunk of a tree. Solid and strong, a tree trunk carries and balances the weight of the branches, even when those branches move and sway in the wind. Similarly, your seat is the foundation of your strength and balance in the saddle: It connects you to your horse. The supplementary aids—the *upper leg*; the *lower leg*; and the *shoulders, arms,* and *hands*—are like the branches of the tree. They can act independent of the seat and of one another, but the seat

3.2
You use your entire body in applying the aids. Your seat acts as the trunk of a tree, while your legs and upper body are the "branches." The branches can act independently, but the trunk remains undisturbed.

remains strong and undisturbed. Ideally, every aid begins with the seat, is controlled by the seat, and finishes with the seat. In other words, the seat constitutes the beginning, middle, and end of every aid. The seat is your "home base."

Here's how the sequence of aids is supposed to work. Begin by inhaling deeply. As you exhale, imagine stretching the top of your head upward and a plumb line being dropped straight down your spine and into the back of the saddle. Your seat bones sink and push down into the saddle and then "scoop" in a forward direction. As your seat bones scoop forward, you close your leg from the hip, through your upper leg, to your knee. Your knee then closes (acting like a hinge between the upper and lower leg), followed by a push of energy from your lower leg. This directs the energy and gives your horse a timing aid for moving forward (fig. 3.3).

Consider this "cycle of energy." Picture the joints of your horse's hind legs bending. His haunches lower; your seat sinks deep into the saddle. The energy runs over his croup and through his gluteal muscles to his stifles; your energy goes from your hips to your knees. His hocks flex; your lower legs lie against his sides, and your heels are down. To keep his haunches active, think of maintaining a dynamic flow of energy from your seat as you press your seat bones down into the saddle; stabilize your body by holding through your upper legs. Close your knees to redirect the energy to your lower legs, which press against his sides and recycle the energy back up to your seat so that the cycle repeats. In essence, it's like a bouncing ball of energy from your seat to your lower legs, and back up to your seat. Your upper leg and knee act as a stabilizer between the lower leg and seat. Realize that, as you do this, your horse activates his haunches in the same way (fig. 3.4).

As you can see, the aids and their function are a bit more complex than the common "seat-leg-hands" concept; and that's why you as a rider must understand your own synonymous athletic development with your horse. For instance, have you ever thought about the fact that your upper and lower legs influence your horse in different ways? The upper leg influences his topline and can make him take a loftier step. When it's closed against his side, the knee tells him to "hold that energy" (in effect, to achieve a level of collection). That's why the knee is used in the half-halt and in downward transitions. The lower leg activates and completes the aids and communicates the desired rhythm, tempo, and timing. As he connects his haunches to his forehand and comes into the bit, your hands and arms receive the energy that you've generated through your seat and cause it to return back to the hindquarters by way of his abdominal muscles.

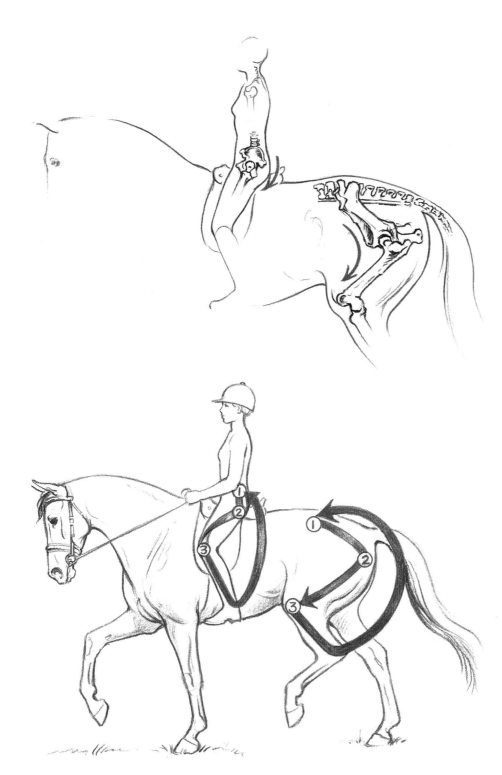

3.3

See how the joints of the horse and rider work together. As you scoop your seat bones forward, your horse reacts and engages the joints in his hind legs.

3.4
The Cycle of Energy
1. *Energy starts in the rider's seat, and activates the horse's haunches.*

2. *Energy then runs from the rider's hips to the inside of her knees, and this influences energy from the horse's gluteal muscles to his stifles.*

3. *The rider's lower legs close and bounce energy back up to her seat as the horse's hocks flex and bounce energy back to his croup.*

Assess Your Understanding

The following questions are designed to test your knowledge and understanding of the purpose of the aids. Compare your responses with the answers on page 107 and give yourself one point for every correct answer.

1. Why should every aid begin and end with the rider's seat?
2. Why are the leg and seat aids used in downward transitions as well as upward ones?
3. In what ways does the rider's upper leg influence the horse?
4. Why are the aids so closely related to the concept of suppleness?
5. What is the role of the rider's hands in aiding the horse?

Score yourself as follows:

5 = Go the head of the class! You have an excellent understanding of the purpose of the aids. Focus your efforts on continuing to refine your aids and their timing and application.

3–4 = You have a well-grounded knowledge of the aids, but some of the fine points need a little polishing. Proceed to the section below, *Set Your Goals*, to develop a strategy for addressing the areas in which your understanding is weak.

0–2 = You may have a rudimentary understanding of the aids, but you need some help in understanding what the various aids do and how they work together. In the *Goals* section next, you'll set realistic objectives for filling in the gaps in your knowledge.

Set Your Goals

In your journal or notebook, write a sentence or two that describes a realistic goal concerning your understanding of the purpose of the aids. Examples:

"I will take longe lessons to improve my seat so that I learn to use my seat and legs to give aids without relying on my hands."

"I will learn to coordinate my aids and to apply them in the proper sequence."

Exercise

For this section, I'm going to use an exercise from t'ai chi that's known as *Push Hands*. You need a partner for this exercise.

EXERCISE: Push Hands

Stand squarely facing your partner, hands at your sides. Have your partner stand facing you and with a hand on each of your hands. Have your partner give you a vigorous push with her left hand while you try to keep your right hand and shoulder from moving. Now, have your partner repeat the push with her left hand; but this time, release your right hand and shoulder and allow them to go where your partner moves them. You'll notice that, if you resist the push, you'll feel tension and resistance in your entire body and maybe lose your balance and have to take a step back when your partner pushes you.. But if you "release," allowing your shoulder to move backward and your partner's hand to go forward, the tension of the push is dissipated and there is no resistance in your body (figs. 3.5 A – C).

The lesson of the *Push Hands* exercise is that horse and rider must "give" to each other; riding can't be a push-and-pull relationship. It's true that, to create a reaction in your horse, you have to apply pressure—but it's what you do with that pressure that makes all the difference.

3.5 A – C
Push Hands Exercise
To start, Jessie and I are facing each other, elbows and knees bent, palms together **(A)**.

We simultaneously push with our left hands. Because we're both relaxed in our arms and shoulders, we're able to maintain our balance. Try to achieve that same centered, give-and-take feeling with the reins as you ride **(B)**.

Repeat the exercise with the right hands pushing **(C)**.

Progress Check

Assess your increased understanding of the purpose of the aids by using the following checklist.

✔ When you watch someone else ride, whether in person or on videotape, can you recognize whether the horse is being suppled properly between the inside and outside aids? Can you recognize instances in which the aids are applied incorrectly, or in which the horse "escapes" to the outside, or "falls" to the inside as a result of unbalanced aids or support from the rider?

✔ When you ride, can you use your aids to keep your horse supple and balanced on a 20-meter circle in both directions without falling in or out on the circle?

✔ *Advanced challenge:* Can you use your aids to keep your horse supple and balanced on a 15-meter circle? A 10-meter circle? An 8-meter circle? Choose the diameter that's appropriate to your horse's level of development and training.

The BODY Element: Flexibility

What You Need to Have

Flexibility gives your body the ability to move in fluid harmony. Some athletic pursuits, such as gymnastics and ballet, demand maximum flexibility—think of the gymnast's work on the uneven bars or the floor, or the ballet dancer's effortless pirouettes and leaps. In comparison, riding requires a narrow range of motion; after all, riders don't move their arms and legs to the limit of their capacity—or at least they're not supposed to! This does not mean, however, that riders don't need to be flexible. To sit apparently effortlessly in the saddle requires a great deal of physical effort and flexibility because your muscles and joints not only have to absorb the shock of your horse's movement; they also must have the strength and flexibility to hold your "form" or position. A rider who appears to be doing nothing—the elegant image that most riders strive to achieve—is actually absorbing a great deal of dynamic movement and energy. Don't believe it? Picture a rider that you've seen who bounces all over the saddle. That person's joints are resistant and stiff, instead of nonresistant, fluid, and working to absorb the shock. The motion has to go somewhere, so it's transmitted through the person's entire body instead.

Betsy's Tips

Make stabilizing your seat your first step toward solving any problem you may encounter while in the saddle.

When you ride, change direction often to work both sides of your horse's body.

Relax the grip on your reins by squeezing and releasing with your fingers.

To help envision the purpose of the inside and outside aids, think of your horse as creating two lines of energy—one along the inside of his body, and one along the outside—as he travels. In what direction are the lines going? If he is supple and balanced, the lines should be parallel. If he is crooked, or off balance, a line will go off in the wrong direction. Your job is to use your aids to bring his lines of energy back on track. On the 20-meter circle, keep his spine directly over that described line. Now imagine building a curved wall on either side of the original line. Your task is to make his body conform to those lines (figs. 3.6 A – C).

3.6 A – C

Seen from the side, this horse and rider are conforming to two parallel lines of energy on the circle **(A)**. *The same picture, as seen from above. Imagine the lines of energy as two walls* **(B)**. *The horse has "crashed" through the imaginary walls, and the rider will need to use her aids to bring the lines of energy back to parallel* **(C)**.

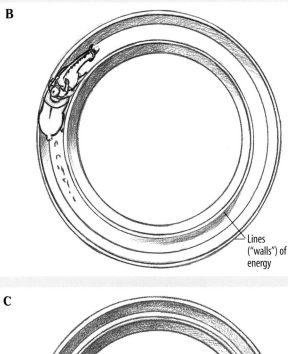

B

Lines ("walls") of energy

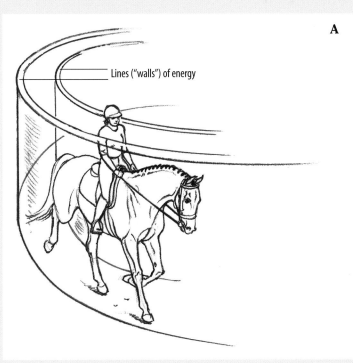

A

Lines ("walls") of energy

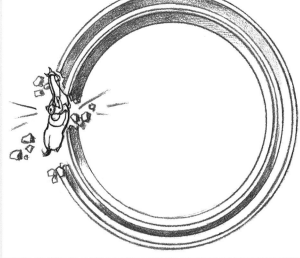

C

If you expect your horse's movements to become more comfortable to sit as his musculature and gymnastic ability develop, you'll actually need to become *more* flexible as he progresses. For example, your back needs to be more flexible to follow the motion of a powerful trot that pushes from behind than to sit that same horse's "warm-up trot," before he really engages his hindquarters and lifts and swings his back. If you are not supple enough, you are likely to have difficulty developing a great deal of true suspension in the strides.

Just as your horse's movement impacts your body, your flexibility (or lack thereof) has a direct effect on his ability to be supple. For comparison, imagine that you're learning how to ski (or, if you're an experienced skier, think back to when you were a beginner). You've been told how to stand, move, turn, and stop—concepts that probably sound pretty simple in theory. But now you're on the slope, poles in hand and skis and bindings attached, and suddenly you're having a hard time remembering what seemed so easy when contemplated in the comfort of your living room. Why? Because your mind and body are tense and "blocked," and you could crash and burn going downhill! You can have a similar effect on your horse, who may well understand what you want but will have a hard time putting it into practice if you're bouncing around on his back. You're giving him too many signals, and it's hard for him to figure out which one to answer. If you're not flexible enough to absorb the shock of his motion and to sit quietly and balanced over his center of gravity, he won't be relaxed, focused, and balanced enough to reach under himself with his hind legs or to stretch down with his neck, even though he physically may be able to do both things.

Assess Your Skill Level

Stand with your back to a wall, legs spread hips' width apart. Think of flattening your back against the wall by pushing your belly button toward your spine. Drop your head, tuck your chin, round your shoulders, and slowly roll down, one vertebra at a time, letting your arms hang. How far can you bend over comfortably while keeping your legs straight?

If you can't get your fingertips much past your knees, you probably would benefit from some work on flexibility. If you can reach nearly to your ankles, you're fairly flexible but could still use some improvement. If you can touch your toes easily, congratulations! You have good functional flexibility. Keep up the good work by incorporating regular flexibility work into your fitness routine.

Set Your Goals

In your journal or notebook, write a sentence or two that describes a realistic goal regarding your flexibility. Examples:

"Each day I will increase my flexibility more and more until I'm able to touch my toes easily."

"I'll spend ten minutes a day doing flexibility exercises in order to maintain my suppleness."

Exercises

Some bodies are naturally more flexible than others, but all of us can improve our flexibility through stretching exercises. Following are six stretching exercises used in *Pilates* that are excellent for suppling the body before and after you ride (fig. 3.7).

As with all physical exercises, start slowly, and don't overdo it. If something hurts, stop and check with your doctor.

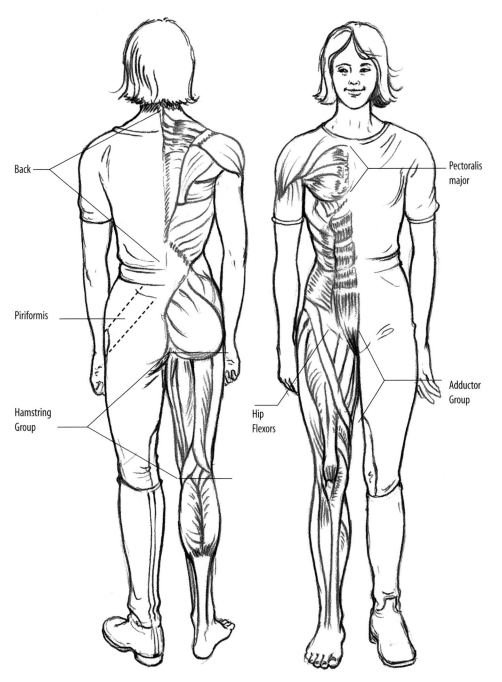

Back

Piriformis

Hamstring
Group

Pectoralis
major

Adductor
Group

Hip
Flexors

3.7
*Muscles used in exercises
in this chapter.*

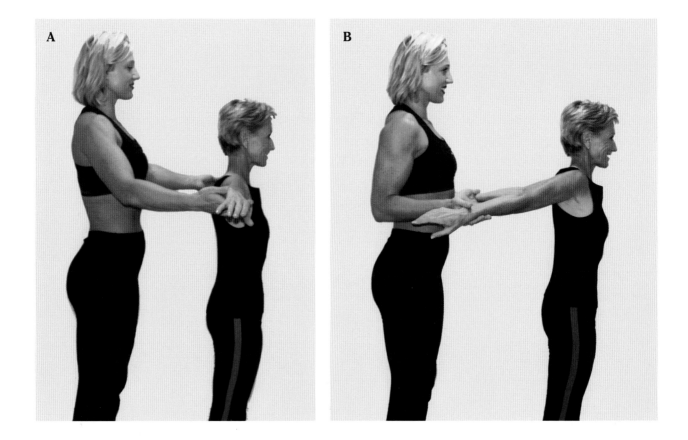

3.8 A & B
Pectoralis Major Stretch
I'm demonstrating the pectoralis-major stretch with Susan Habanova assisting. This photo shows the starting position: with my arms extended to the sides, parallel to the floor, and Susan gently grasping my wrists **(A)**.

Now, the stretch: Susan gently takes my arms back until I feel a comfortable stretch **(B)**.

EXERCISE 1: Pectoralis Major Stretch

This stretch will help to eliminate tightness in the chest. As you stretch the front of your chest, you will help to straighten your rounded shoulders and to realign your head over your shoulders.

You can do this stretch with a partner or by yourself, using a door frame. Start by standing tall and extending your arms straight out to your sides. If you are working with a partner, have him or her gently take both of your arms back until you feel a comfortable stretch (tell your partner to stop if your arms go back too far for comfort). If you are working alone, place your arms on either side of a door frame and walk forward until you feel a stretch. As you stretch, inhale and *axially elongate* and *engage your core* (see p. 34). If you do this exercise correctly, you will feel a stretch across the front of your chest. Hold the stretch for fifteen seconds and release. Repeat twice (figs. 3.8 A & B).

I'm demonstrating the back stretch over an exercise ball. I've allowed my legs to hang down and have rolled along the ball until I feel a nice stretch in my lower back.

EXERCISE 2: Back Stretch Over a Ball

Exercise balls (also known as Swiss balls or sport balls) are versatile and inexpensive pieces of fitness equipment and are available from most physical therapists and fitness-equipment suppliers as well as from many fitness and chiropractic facilities and yoga and fitness catalogs. Balls come in various diameters; your thighs should be parallel to the floor when you sit on the properly inflated ball.

Using a ball is an excellent and safe way to stretch your back and to relieve any tightness or discomfort caused by riding. (If you experience constant or worsening back pain, see your doctor.)

To do this exercise, lie face down over the ball and slowly roll forward until your hands reach the ground. Allow your legs to hang down, which will create a traction-like stretch. Adjust your position until you find the one that best stretches your lower back. Breathe normally as you stretch (fig. 3.9).

3.10
Piriformis Stretch
Beginner piriformis stretch: I'm stretching my right outer thigh and buttock region while keeping my left leg bent.

3.11
More advanced piriformis stretch: By straightening my left leg after crossing my right ankle over my left knee, I've achieved a more intense stretch.

EXERCISE 3: Piriformis Stretch

Many of us spend most of our waking hours in a seated position, which tends to tighten the *piriformis* muscles—the lateral thigh muscles that rotate the hips outward. This tightness can be counterproductive for riding because, in order to achieve the internal rotation of the hips required for riding, the piriformis muscles must be flexible enough to allow the hips to rotate inward.

Start by lying on your back with your right knee bent and your feet on the floor. Raise your left leg and cross your left ankle over your right knee, keeping your pelvis in a neutral position (rotated neither forward nor backward). Relax and allow your left knee to rotate outward; you should feel a stretch on the outer thigh and buttock region of your left leg. Hold the stretch for fifteen seconds and release. For a more intense stretch, straighten your right leg toward the ceiling after you cross your left ankle over your right knee, and hold onto your right leg with your hands behind your knee. Stretch two more times; then repeat the exercise with your right leg (figs. 3.10 and 3.11).

3.12 A & B
Adductor Stretch
The adductor (inner thigh) stretch: Susan shows the starting position **(A)**.

The adductor stretch: Susan is extremely flexible in her body; don't be discouraged if you can't stretch all the way down to the floor as she has here. Stretch down only as far as you can go while keeping your legs straight and your seat bones anchored to the floor **(B)**.

EXERCISE 4: Adductor (Inner Thigh) Stretch

Sit comfortably with both of your seat bones on the floor and your legs opened as wide as possible. As you exhale, draw your core into your spine. Place your hands in front of you for support, and begin to lean forward until you feel a comfortable stretch. Hold the stretch for fifteen seconds. Inhale and roll up slowly, using your core muscles more than your back. Repeat twice (figs. 3.12 A & B).

3.13 A & B
Hamstring Stretch
Susan and I demonstrate the hamstring stretch with a partner. Here, I'm in the starting position, ready to stretch my left leg **(A)**.

Susan gently takes my leg back until I feel the stretch in my left hamstring **(B)**.

EXERCISE 5: Hamstring Stretch

This exercise can be done alone or with a partner. If you do not have a partner, you'll need a sturdy bath towel.

If you're working alone, loop the towel around your left foot and grasp the ends in each hand. Lie on your back with both legs straight on the floor. Slowly raise your left leg until you feel a comfortable stretch. (If you're working with a partner, have him or her gently raise your left leg while holding it straight.) Hold the stretch for fifteen seconds; then repeat with your right leg (figs. 3.13 A & B).

EXERCISE 6: Hip Flexor Stretch

Lie on your right side with your left leg bent, and hold on to your left ankle with your left hand. "Stack" your hips over each other and engage your core so there is no arch in your back. Keep your right leg bent and in front of you for support. Exhale and use your left hand to take your left hip backward until you feel a stretch along the front of your left hip. Keep your spine straight as you take your hip back, and do not arch your back. Take your hip back until you feel the stretch, and hold the stretch for 15 seconds two times. Repeat with the other leg (figs. 3.14 A & B).

3.14 A & B
Hip Flexor Stretch
Starting position for the right hip flexor stretch **(A)**.

I've drawn my right hip back with my right arm until I feel the stretch along the front of the hip **(B)**.

3.15 A – D
Rolling Down the Wall

To start, I'm standing very straight against a wall with my core muscles engaged and my feet together **(A)**.

Beginning with my head and neck, I begin rolling down the wall one vertebra at a time. To keep my balance at this point (it's harder than you think!), I focus on keeping my abdominal muscles lifted **(B & C)**.

After I've rolled down as far as is comfortable, I use my abdominal muscles to initiate the rolling-up process, one vertebra at a time, until I'm back in my starting position **(D)**.

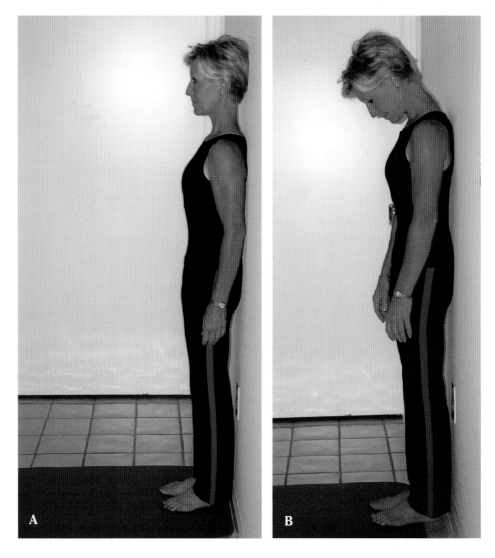

EXERCISE 7: Rolling Down the Wall

This exercise is a great way to end any kind of training session or workout. Stand with your back against a wall and your feet together and about eight to ten inches from the base of the wall. Inhale and slowly roll down, one vertebra at a time, only as far as you can while keeping your tailbone in contact with the wall. Let your arms hang down. Roll back up the wall, one vertebra at a time, and end by exhaling and pressing your spine against the wall (figs. 3.15 A – D).

Progress Check

It's easy to tell whether you've improved at the touch-your-toes stretching exercise, but measuring flexibility in other ways can be nebulous. The best way to assess your progress is to consider whether you feel an improved ease of movement—a sort of increased comfort and fluidity in your own skin. Ask yourself:

 ✔ Do I feel as if the movements of my body have become easier and more graceful?

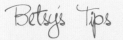

Betsy's Tips

If you feel discomfort, stiffness, or unevenness as you ride, chances are that you are tensing in one or more areas of your body. Work on heightening your self-awareness as you ride; monitor how your body feels during the session. Start applying the fitness principles as you ride. If you become aware of tension or discomfort, try to figure out the cause. Some riders try to counterbalance a horse's stiff side by tightening the shoulder on the opposite side; if you find yourself doing this, focus on keeping your shoulders back and down and your hips and shoulders parallel to your horse's hips and shoulders. Continually go through a mental checklist and rebalance your position. In other cases, rider tension is caused by lack of strength. Weak in an area of the body that needs to be strong for riding—such as the seat (the lower back, abdominal and gluteal muscles, and upper legs)—the rider may unconsciously try to compensate by "holding" with the shoulders, the arms, or a clutching leg. Such weakness, particularly in the abdominal muscles, is the reason that many riders suffer from back pain.

✔ Am I feeling stronger and more flexible than I did ten days ago? A month ago?

✔ In the saddle, do I feel as if my joints are bending and flexing to absorb my horse's movement more than they were ten days ago? A month ago?

✔ Does my horse become suppler during the course of our schooling sessions? If he does, am I aware of the relationship between his suppleness and the suppleness in my body?

✔ Does my horse stay equally supple and balanced, with the same amount of bend, when I ride a figure-of-eight with dimensions appropriate to his level of training?

The SPIRIT Element: Relaxation and Flow

What You Need to Be

The dictionary definitions of *relaxation* include "abatement or relief from work, effort, etc." and "a loosening or slackening." The relevant definition of *flow* is "to proceed continuously and smoothly." In equestrian terms, I think of relaxation and flow as a state in which you react in a very level, unemotional way to your horse and your training. You don't take things personally. You move mentally with your horse; you don't fight him; you ask and then wait and see what he offers in response. You ask for something and *allow* him to respond; then you react to his response from a very steady, calm place.

If you have a relaxed attitude about your riding and your relationship with your horse, you regard your training sessions as inspired and enjoyable, and you're able to see past the occasional difficult session without getting bogged down with negativity and self-doubt. You're not locked into one way of thinking or acting. You "let it be." You are not "blocked," either physically or mentally. Most "blockages" are defense mechanisms against fear. For instance, some riders hold one rein relentlessly, despite their instructors' constant nagging to "Let go of that right rein." The rider won't let go because the horse is pulling and she thinks she might be run away with if she relaxes her iron grip on the rein—which, more often than not, causes the horse to pull even harder. Paradoxically, if the rider would let go, the horse probably also would let go and stop pulling because you have just released the tension.

To be able to "go with the flow" of your horse, you have to develop the knack of coming to a peaceful and still place in your mind where nothing can distract you. To do so, you have to let go of all of the outside influences and worries in your life: the tensions of the day, the onlookers at the horse show, the fears that your horse will spook or misbehave. Train yourself to shut out any negative thoughts and to let them go. Guard your thoughts, and have trust and faith in your training.

Tension and worry in your mind transforms into tension and stiffness in your body, and that's why relaxation and flow are the psychological component of the goal of suppleness. Let me give you a few examples. A rider who is bothered by everything external is going to have a very nervous horse. If you tense up every time a tractor passes, a horse walks by, or a dog runs into the arena, you're effectively communicating to your horse that these things are worrisome and that he should worry, too. At a horse show, if you're worried about your competitors or the spectators or the judge, you're wasting valuable time by focusing your energies and thoughts on external factors that you can't control instead of the one factor that you can control: your thoughts while riding. In both cases, unless you "let go," your mental and physical tension will cause your horse to begin to protect his own body; even the most supple horse will probably lose his *losgelassenheit* within minutes. In contrast, "letting go" mentally and coming to a place of quietness in your mind causes your body to relax and, as a result, to become more flexible and much more enjoyable.

Assess Your Psyche

Do any of the following happen to you on a regular basis? If so, you'll want to put some energy into relaxing and "going with the flow."

1. I often feel tense or anxious when it's time to go to the barn and ride.
2. I have difficulty following my horse's motion when I ride; the motion seems very jarring.
3. I often feel physical stiffness, discomfort, or tension while I'm riding.
4. I'm afraid to relax and let go because I fear my horse will take off or buck.
5. I don't really trust my horse.
6. When I ride, I'm easily distracted.
7. My horse is tense and spooky.

Set Your Goals

In your journal or notebook, write a sentence or two that describes a realistic goal regarding relaxation and flow. Examples:

"I will discuss my riding anxieties with my instructor. I will get his or her opinion as to the cause of my fears. If I'm over-mounted, I will discuss my options. If my horse isn't the problem, we will formulate a strategy for carefully and safely helping me to push through my comfort zone."

"I will learn to realize when I am becoming tense, and I will develop relaxation strategies."

"My goal is to improve my ability to focus on the task at hand and not to be distracted by outside factors."

Exercises

EXERCISE 1: Visualization and Focus

Visualization is a highly effective performance-enhancement technique that's commonly used by elite athletes. Its effectiveness is due to the fact that your mind does not know the difference between an actual response and a visualized response. When you visualize yourself performing in a certain way, your brain sends impulses to the muscles involved, just as if you were actually going through the motions. As a result, you gain "muscle memory" of those actions.

The key to successful visualization is *detail*. Choose a riding-related scenario that's been causing you problems or anxiety. It can be as narrow as a specific movement or as broad as an upcoming clinic or test at the next horse show. Now imagine that you're working on that movement or that you're at that clinic or show. Picture in your mind the setting—the sights, sounds, and smells; the feel of your horse underneath you, and the reins in your hands. If you're at a show, picture the spectators and hear the announcer's calls. Fill in every detail until it seems as if you've actually been transported to the scene, or that you're watching a videotape of the event.

As you visualize, various thoughts will pop into your head—perhaps negative thoughts. Let them come in. Don't suppress negative thoughts; instead, allow yourself to have them, think about how you'll handle them, and then let them go right out again and get back to the positives—to what you want to have happen. Accept the negatives or challenges as part of the experience, but learn how to let them go and stay realistic. After all, unplanned and unwanted things do happen when we're riding: Our horses make mistakes, or the judge's umbrella blows over, or a horse in the next ring gets loose. The important thing is to deal with those possibilities if they come up during the visualization; then, if something happens during the ride, you'll be prepared because you've already dealt with the situation mentally.

Let me give you an example of how I think it through. I'm visualizing riding a test on the stallion Hilltop's Giotto, a horse that I know likes to come to a rather abrupt halt. I don't want him to halt that way, and so I think about it during my visualization. The first couple of times, I visualize him halting abruptly. Next, I think to myself that I'm going to correct that halt. I go through the corrections in my mind; I know that I've got to collect him a little more, say, six strides before I come to the halt. He lowers his haunches, and we come into the halt with the collection coming up into my hands; I get softer in my back; I keep my seat connected to his back so that it stays up underneath me; I use my legs a little more; I make him stay with me until the very last stride. Then he halts abruptly, so I ride the center-line-and-halt again in my mind (fig. 3.16). This time, I stay a little stronger through the last moment to finish it. Perfect. Then I do it again in my mind several more times, allowing what happens to come in, correcting it, making it better and better until I feel that it's perfect. Now I have a picture—a "feel."

Whatever you fear may happen, you must correct it in your mind before you can correct it on your horse. Then, in the actual situation, you've done it so many times in your mind that you *know* how to correct it because you've trained yourself to do so. There are no surprises.

Now that you know how detailed your visualization needs to be, try your own.

EXERCISE 2: Reduce Stress Through Breathing

Another very easy and instantaneous way to achieve relaxation and flow during a stressful moment is simply to take a deliberate, deep breath. Inhale deeply; and as you exhale, think "let go" and feel yourself relaxing. Practice this exercise often so that you can claim it as your own when you need it most.

3.16

Visualization

See yourself on your horse, riding your dressage test or whatever exercise it is that you're working on. Think through any possible challenges, and mentally correct them.

Progress Check

Test the effectiveness of your unmounted work with a simple mounted exercise. As always, your horse will serve as a barometer of your progress—he'll let you know, through his actions and attitude, whether your efforts at relaxation are working.

- ✔ On a 20-meter circle (or smaller—choose the diameter that's appropriate to your horse's level of training), can you walk, trot, and canter in both directions for ten minutes while he remains supple and relaxed? If so, you're ready to move on. If not, continue with your relaxation exercises and recheck your progress every week to ten days.
- ✔ Try your breathing exercise. Practice it over and over until you can see and feel definite results.

Betsy's Tips

If riding in clinics or shows makes you nervous, the best "cure" is—to borrow from the well-known *Nike*-commercial line—"just do it." There's no substitute for actually getting out there and going through it to teach you that you can do it, that people are not going to laugh at you, and that much of your anxiety was self-produced. Ask yourself: What's the worst that can happen? Usually, it's not bad at all!

Some instructors hold mock shows for their anxious students. They get a group of people together to serve as spectators, they install a judge's booth and a judge at "C," and they have their students braid up, dress up, and ride through their tests. The experience helps some riders to overcome their fears about riding in front of others and also accustoms them to showing routines and protocol. It's also good to have some spectators during your lessons. You'll learn that making a mistake doesn't hurt.

Of course, the "just do it" approach is appropriate only if your fears are of the performance-jitters variety. Forcing yourself (or allowing an instructor to bully you) to do something that scares you and that carries some risk, such as jumping a cross-country course, usually does not overcome your fears and may even put you at risk of injury. If you're truly terrified of jumping cross-country, you may want to ask yourself whether you really need to do that in order to reach your riding goals. If you're determined to overcome your fears, find an extra-patient instructor who will work with you slowly and carefully, one baby step at a time.

HORSE
THE *supple* HORSE

The MIND Element: Yields to the Leg

What Your Horse Needs to Know

After your horse learns to go forward in rhythm, he needs to learn that your legs can tell him to move sideways as well as forward. He must understand the difference between what the German National Equestrian Federation's official handbook calls a "forward driving leg aid," which asks the horse to move straight forward; and a "forward/sideways driving leg aid," which "causes the hind leg on that side to move forward/sideways away from the leg giving the aid."[3] All turns and lateral movements require the horse to yield to the leg.

What your horse needs to understand is that the rider's leg serves as a support and a direction; it indicates to him where his hind leg is supposed to go. When he understands that, you can put him any place you want him. He must accept the leg and learn that the leg is not something for him to go against and resist. If he resists yielding to the leg, he is working against the direction that you want for him to go. He has to learn to work together with the leg.

Some horses are more inclined than others to yield to the leg with little fuss. Like people, some horses are domineering by nature, while others are more submissive. Watch any group of young horses playing in the field. If one pushes another, does he move over softly, or does he kick out in protest? The horse that reacts assertively is likely to push back against your leg when he starts training. You, the rider, need to understand his personality and to work with him to teach him, quietly and in a nonthreatening, nonabusive way, that you are the boss and you make the decisions.

Assess Your Horse's Understanding

The simple self-tests below will give you a good idea of how well your horse understands (and accepts) yielding to the leg.

1. From the ground, does your horse move over promptly and willingly if you give him a gentle nudge in the side?

2. Mounted, does your horse know how to do a turn on the forehand? That is, will he pivot with his hind legs away from your leg while keeping his front legs almost in place?

3. Does your horse know how to do a leg-yield? That is, will he step forward and sideways away from your inside leg at the walk and at the trot?

4. If you answered no to any of the above, your energy needs to be directed toward your horse's understanding (or acceptance) of the "forward/sideways driving leg aid."

Set Your Goals

In your journal or notebook, write a sentence or two that describes a realistic 30-day goal regarding your horse's understanding of the concept of yielding to the leg. Examples:

"I will teach my horse that he must continue to go forward while he moves sideways."

"I will teach my horse that pushing back against my leg is not acceptable. He must step over when I ask."

Exercises

First, I'll give you an exercise that's useful in teaching a horse to yield to the leg. Then I'll give you a two-person exercise that's effective for overcoming the resistance of a stubborn or "directionally challenged" horse.

EXERCISE 1: Help with Basic Leg-Yielding

Use the wall of the arena to help guide your horse in the desired direction. Start on the left rein. On the long side, push his haunches to the inside, remaining at a slight angle (about 30 degrees) to the wall or fence line. His forehand will remain on the track, while his haunches will move inward, off the track. Practice this for a few strides at a time down the long side; then ask him to walk forward by pushing forward with your seat and closing your upper legs, pressing strongly with your right upper leg toward your left rein to straighten him. Keep your upper body straight and aligned over your hips and heels; your shoulders should be aligned with his shoulders. Move his haunches over again to the left. If he does not yield, reinforce your leg aid with the use of your whip. Keep your knees in place to give form and

3.17 A & B

In the walk, I am leg-yielding Manhattan away from my right leg along the long side of the arena. Note that his body is straight, with just a slight amount of flexion to the right, away from the direction of travel **(A)**.

He then repeats the exercise in the opposite direction. Notice how I am able to relax on the inside left rein as Manhattan accepts the contact on the outside right rein **(B)**.

definition to the movement. Maintain contact with the left rein while positioning his nose slightly to the right. As he steps over with his hind legs, be sensitive in your hands and look for moments that you can relax your hold of the reins to let him reach into your hands. Straighten him for a stride or two; then repeat the exercise until he's leg-yielded about ten to fifteen meters down the long side. Change directions and practice the leg-yield on the right hand, making him active and responsive to your left leg. After he's able to maintain his balance while obediently leg-yielding along the wall in the walk, try the same exercise at the trot. As he gains confidence and balance, increase the trot strides until he's traveling at his normal working pace (figs. 3.17 A & B).

EXERCISE 2: For the Confused or Stubborn Horse

You'll need a knowledgeable helper—your instructor would be ideal—for this exercise. Begin by walking straight ahead along the quarter line of the arena. Have a helper walk next to you on your horse's left side, near the girth. Your helper should keep her body positioned parallel to your horse, stepping along with your horse and taking care not to stand back near his hindquarters in case he kicks out. For her safety, she must remain aware of the movements of your horse's hindquarters at all times.

Position your horse for the leg-yield to the right, toward the track. Ask him to step forward and sideways with your left leg. Have your helper reinforce your aids by nudging your horse behind the girth with her hand as if she were asking him to move over. If he resists, ask again and have your helper push him sideways a bit more forcefully. It should not take much force to nudge him over. If you still get resistance, walk straight forward for a few strides, then ask again for the leg-yield with your helper's assistance. If your horse takes even one step forward and sideways with his inside hind leg, soften your hands and legs and praise him. Be happy with small victories, and be sure to praise your horse when he yields so that he gets the idea that stepping forward and sideways is what you want. If he resists, calmly and firmly repeat the exercise until he understands that he must yield his haunches to your leg. Your helper can literally push him sideways and give him a clearer idea of what you want if he doesn't understand right away.

Progress Check

Use the following checklist to assess your horse's improvement.

- ✔ If you needed a ground person to help move your horse over, can you now get at least a few steps of leg-yield without your helper's reinforcement?
- ✔ If your horse was inclined to push back against your leg or to kick out at the leg, does he now step over promptly and willingly?
- ✔ Does your horse yield to the leg equally well on both sides?

Betsy's Tips

As you work on developing your horse's understanding that he must yield to the leg, keep in mind that his body mirrors your own in almost all cases. A supple rider on a stiff horse has a good chance of producing a supple horse; in turn, a stiff rider on a supple horse will produce a stiff horse.

Also, be sure to align your body correctly as you ride; if you're crooked, you'll disrupt your horse's balance, and a horse that's having to compensate in his own body for his unbalanced rider cannot be supple. Be sure not to lean to one side or the other with your upper body, and keep your weight even into both seat bones. When you want your horse to take a step forward and sideways, put a little extra weight into the seat bone on the side to which you want him to move by staying heavy in your seat. Take care that your upper body stays directly over your hips. Then step a bit more heavily into that inside stirrup, your upper legs supporting and directing his motion where you want it to go—inside lower leg on the girth, outside leg behind the girth and pushing over. He'll naturally want to step underneath your weight to balance himself. Have the feeling that you "aim" your upper legs securely in the direction you want to go, and expect your horse to follow (figs. 3.18 A – C).

A

3. 18 A – C

Correct Alignment: I'm sitting in the middle of the saddle, with a straight line from my head, down my spine, and to my tailbone. My weight is distributed evenly in both seat bones and in both stirrups. I could have a little more weight in the left stirrup **(A)**.

B

C

In this photo I've collapsed my left hip. This has caused my head, shoulders, elbows, and spine to become crooked. I'm no longer sitting evenly on both seat bones, so there's too much weight in my right stirrup and not enough in my left **(B)**.

My position here may not look as disharmonious as in the previous photo, but look carefully: Although my upper body is fairly well aligned, I'm sitting too far to the right in the saddle instead of keeping my seat centered. My horse will have a hard time maintaining his own balance and will probably tend to drift right as he attempts to stabilize himself underneath my off-center weight **(C)**.

The BODY Element: Fluency and Flexibility

What Your Horse Needs to Have

When a horse's joints do not flex, he is not in lateral balance. As a result, he moves inefficiently, not just behind but throughout his entire body. Such a horse may become frustrated because he's not able to carry out his rider's commands.

The *Training Pyramid* is such a useful guide because it so clearly illustrates the way that each level of understanding and development lays the foundation for the ones to follow. At this stage of training, suppleness achieved and leg-yielding and bending exercises are setting the stage for the next building block, which is acceptance of rein contact. As your horse learns to bend and give throughout his body and to yield to the leg, he's also allowing you to push him into the contact with the bit. If his body is not flexible and he is not able to move in a smooth, fluent fashion, it will be very difficult to get him to accept contact.

At this stage of training, you're building on the longitudinal development that you began when you first worked on establishing a regular rhythm and tempo and to teach your horse to go forward from your seat and leg. Now, as you develop your horse's suppleness, you're combining his longitudinal development with lateral suppleness, and you're working toward establishing contact.

Assess Your Horse's Skill Level

To get a clear picture of your horse's level of fluency and flexibility, do the following gymnastic exercises and ask yourself the accompanying questions. Ask your instructor or a knowledgeable ground person for his or her opinions if you're not sure of the answers.

1. Can your horse bend evenly in both directions and remain balanced and in a consistent rhythm and tempo on a three-loop serpentine at the trot?
2. Can your horse leg-yield at the walk and the trot, maintaining a steady rhythm in both directions?

All horses have a strong side and a weak side (just as we're either right-handed or left-handed), and so all naturally tend to be more flexible in one direction. Your job is to strengthen his weak side and stretch his strong side through gymnastic exercises so that he's able to move equally fluently in both directions. So be sure that, as you work to bend your horse on a curved line, you not only think of the bend to the inside but also are concerned with the stretch on the outside of his body.

Set Your Goals

In your journal or notebook, write a sentence or two that describes a realistic 30-day goal regarding your horse's fluency and flexibility. Examples:

"Day by day, I will improve my horse's ability to bend to the right so that he can bend in that direction as easily as he bends to the left."

"I will increase the fluency of my horse's movement so that he does not lose forwardness or rhythm when he changes bend or direction."

"My horse will yield to my leg easily."

"I'll be sure to work on stretching his muscles on the outside of the bend as well as to work him longitudinally from his haunches, over his back and neck, and reaching toward my hands."

Exercise

EXERCISE: Spiral-in/Leg-yield Out on the Circle

This exercise is one of my all-time favorites, and I use it with all of my own horses as well as in my clinics (fig. 3.19).

Begin by establishing a 20-meter circle to the left in working trot rising. After you've achieved a good rhythm, sit the trot. (If your horse is less advanced, you may choose to remain in the rising trot.) Gradually, meter by meter, decrease the circumference of the circle to fifteen meters by leg-yielding inward. (On a more advanced horse, leg-yield inward to a ten-meter circle.)

To ride the leg-yield, start by defining a good connection to your right rein and taking a slight counter-bend to the right. Keep your head up, stretch up through your spine, and square your shoulders. Make sure that your seat is balanced in the saddle as you push more heavily into your right seat bone. Actively close and tighten your right upper leg against the saddle from your hip to your knee, and push your upper leg toward the left rein. As your horse moves his shoulders to the left, support that movement by closing your left upper leg: Feel as though you're pulling both knees to the left. To keep his strides forward and active, push with your seat and close your lower legs as he brings his shoulders in front of his haunches and

3.19

Spiral-in/Leg-yield Out on the Circle

1. Gradually, spiral inward in a leg-yield—meter by meter—to a 15- or 10-meter circle, the size depends on your horse's level. It is important to keep your horse within the circle lines.

2. Stay on the smaller circle until your horse is balanced, then carefully change his flexion and leg-yield back out on the circle.

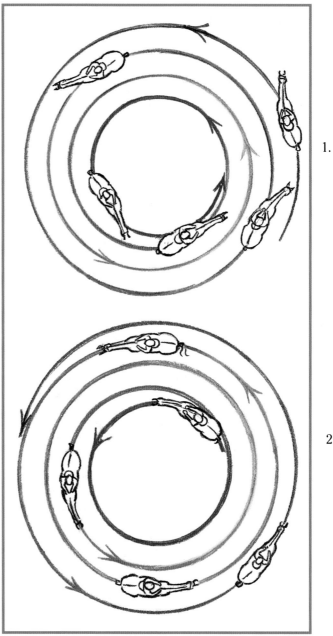

1.

2.

to the left. Feel the connection between your right leg and your left rein. Think of his hip and shoulder as coming closer together on the outside as he moves forward and sideways.

After you have decreased the size of the circle the desired amount (to ten meters or fifteen meters), stay on that circle until your horse is balanced and you can change the bend from a counter-bend right to a steady bend to the left. The challenge here is to make sure that his hoof prints stay exactly on the same circle as you change the bend in his body from right to left. Now, with your horse in true bend, guide him back out to the 20-meter circle by leg-yielding back to the outside, reversing the same sequence of aids that you used for the leg-yield in. His inside hip and shoulder will now be closer together. Your energy flows as follows:

> From the top of your head.

> Down your spine.

> Into the back of your seat and upper legs.

> Securing your knees and pushing with your lower legs, which circulate the energy back up to your seat and forward into your massaging inner fingers (which in turn create the balance).

> Into the outside rein.

After your horse can handle the exercise comfortably in the trot, increase the difficulty of the exercise by incorporating transitions from trot to canter. In the sitting trot, leg-yield in from a 20-meter circle to a fifteen-meter circle, pushing him inward with the same energy from your seat into your outside leg and rein. When he is in rhythm and balanced on the fifteen-meter circle, begin to leg-yield outward and, making sure that he remains in balance, ask him to pick up the true (inside) canter lead about halfway out on the circle, through the leg-yield. Circle once or twice around at the canter in true bend, make a transition to the trot, and spiral in again on the circle in leg-yield. The transition from trot to canter is always made while going *out* on the circle. During your leg-yield work, think of yielding one meter, going forward one meter, yielding one meter, going forward one meter, and so on.

Spiral in by decreasing the size of the circle *gradually*, meter by meter, until you've reduced the size of the circle to fifteen or ten meters (choose the appropriate diameter for your horse's level of training). The goal as you spiral in is to bring the line from his haunches to his forehand closer together on the outside as you

Betsy's Tips

As you school the spiraling-in portion of the suppling exercise, imagine that you're in a pool of water. I'm standing in the middle of the circle, pulling your horse in by his saddle pad. Envisioning his ribcage coming in first (before his shoulders and hips) will help to keep his shoulders and haunches aligned correctly on the circle. Always think of keeping his feet on the 20-meter circle; only the bend in his body changes.

During both the spiraling-in and leg-yielding-out phases, count aloud as the meters decrease or increase: "Twenty… nineteen…eighteen…" and so on. Take your time! Don't rush or "fall" inward; balance inward. Counting aloud will make you more aware of the speed at which you're moving out or in and will help prevent you from coming in or out so quickly that your horse is unable to maintain his balance and "falls" onto his inside or outside shoulder with his hindquarters trailing or his shoulder leading.

This is a difficult exercise; but if you're patient, I'm sure that you'll find it beneficial throughout your training.

spiral inward. As you spiral outward, your goal is to shorten the distance between his inside hip and his shoulder. To do this correctly is extremely difficult; you'll probably find that either his shoulders or his haunches want to come in first.

When you've spiraled in to your smaller circle, simply change the flexion in your horse's neck and the bend in his body; but don't let his feet move off the arc of the circle. Position your horse slightly to the inside with your inside rein and leg for a couple of revolutions. Then, maintaining inside flexion, ask him to leg-yield out on the circle, meter by meter, until you're back on your original 20-meter circle. Again, pay special attention to the alignment of his shoulders and haunches to maintain his alignment on the arc of the circle (figs. 3.20 A – E).

You'll know your horse is doing this exercise correctly when he's able to maintain his rhythm, tempo, and alignment during the spiraling-in and the leg-yielding out; and when he changes his flexion and bend fluently in preparation for the leg-yield out. You'll find that this exercise can be used, along with other circle variations, throughout all of your training (figs 3.21 A & B, 3.22 A & B, and 3.23).

Progress Check

As you work on the spiraling-in/leg-yielding-out exercise, assess your horse's progress with the following tests:

✔ Can you bring your horse's hip and shoulder closer together as you spiral in and out on the circle while your horse stays balanced and supple?

✔ Can you change the flexion of your horse's neck and the bend in his body from outside to inside without his moving off the circle yet remaining balanced and supple?

3.20 A – E
Spiral-in/Leg-yield Out on the Circle
Working from an energetic trot on a 20-meter circle, I begin to get flexion to the right into my outside rein by driving with my right leg **(A)**.

I begin taking the first spiraling step inward to the left (toward the center of the circle) **(B)**.

Continued:

3.20 A – E (cont.)
*I use my seat to indicate that we are now going to spiral out, and I re-establish a slight flexion to the left (**C**).*

*As I come back to center in my seat, Manhattan begins to cross over with his inside hind leg, spiraling out on a circle (**D**).*

E

Leg-yield is complete. The result creates a more supple body in the horse **(E)**.

Rider's Tip: *As you begin lateral movements, continue to stay stable in your hips.*

3.21 A & B

A correct circle. The horse's body matches the arc of the circle. By conforming to the lateral bend of the circle, the distance from the horse's inside hip to his inside shoulder shortens, and the distance from his outside hip to outside shoulder, lengthens **(A)**.

Incorrect. The horse's body is not conforming to the circle's arc **(B)**.

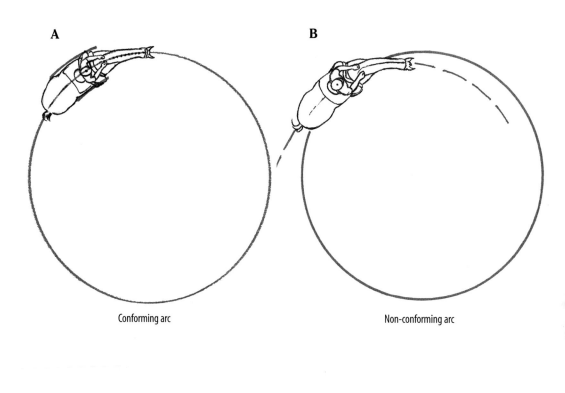

A   B

Conforming arc   Non-conforming arc

3.22 A & B

Lateral-bend exercises. The shoulder-in brings the line of the forehand to the inside of the circle **(A)**.

The haunches-in brings the line of the haunches to the inside of the circle **(B)**.

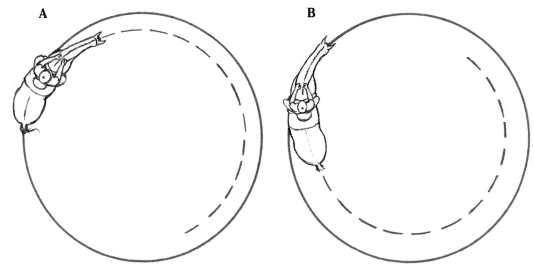

A   B

Shoulder-in   Haunches-in

The SPIRIT Element: Willingness

What Your Horse Needs to Be

Willingness is an innate quality. If your horse is willing, he'll give you the feeling that he enjoys his work and that he wants to please you. A willing horse is happy and energetic and looks forward to his sessions with you; he doesn't regard them as a chore (fig. 3.24). This is a joy! I think of willingness as being part of intention. Is he willing? Does he intend to work for you?

Willingness manifests itself in your horse's behavior on the ground as well as when he's being ridden. A horse that's willing and eager to work is pleased to see you: He'll cheerfully walk up to you in the stall or in the paddock, and in most cases he acts relaxed and happy while he's being groomed and tacked up. An unwilling horse, on the other hand, may turn his hind end to you, pin his ears, act grumpy, or even nip or kick at you as you work around him. Realize, however, that some very willing horses don't like vigorous brushing, too-tight girths, and other strong sensations. That's sensitivity, not necessarily unwillingness.

3.24
*Portrait of willingness: a happy horse
who likes his job and wants to please.*

Willingness becomes important at this stage of training because suppleness requires acceptance and relaxation, and an unwilling horse has neither of these. Resentment of the rider's leg, annoyance at being touched and handled, dislike of his work—all create a tense, unhappy horse that's not going to take kindly to being asked to acquiesce to his rider's requests. As a trainer, I also want to see willingness at this time in a horse's development because a willing horse will work with me later on in his training when I begin asking him for more difficulty. If he's resistant at this early stage, I'm going to have a great challenge when I try to train him to do things that require more intense aids, more leg, and more from him physically and mentally.

True willingness is more than obedience and a strong work ethic. An obedient horse will do what you ask of him, whether he wants to or not. A horse with a good work ethic thinks that it's okay to go to work; he's not thinking up ways to get out of work. But a willing horse combines obedience and a work ethic with the desire to do his job. He doesn't just do his job because he likes to work; he does his job because he loves what he does.

Some horses are innately more willing than others, just as some people are innately more passionate and driven. The horse that is born willing is a sheer joy and much easier to train than the horse that only wants to graze in the pasture and doesn't care about pleasing you. However, even a willing horse's good attitude can be spoiled through abuse or bad training; and horses, like people, do have opinions about what kinds of work they like and dislike. A horse's level of willingness can be increased through careful training, and in a moment, I'll give you some simple strategies that have been successful for me. But part of your task in addressing this *spirit* element is to ask yourself whether your horse is happy in the career that you've chosen for him. As you'll see in *Assess Your Horse's Psyche* below, it is not uncommon for a horse to undergo a radical personality transformation when he's finally allowed to do the job that's best suited to *his* mind, body, and spirit.

Assess Your Horse's Psyche

Assessing your horse's willingness is a two-step process. You'll be seeking the answers to the following questions:

1. What is my horse's overall level of willingness at this point in his life?

2. What is his level of willingness—in other words, his psychological suit-ability—regarding my chosen discipline?

3. Does my horse like what he's doing? Does he love what he's doing?

Overall willingness. Ask yourself the following series of questions, and be hon-est with yourself in your responses. You love your horse, but in order to work with him in the most effective and kind manner you have to see him as an individual, with a realistic picture of his physical and psychological strengths, weaknesses, and quirks. Realize that there is no such thing as the "perfect" horse, just as there is no such thing as a perfect human being.

If you think that you might have difficulty performing a realistic assessment, whether due to inexperience or lack of perspective, ask your instructor or a knowl-edgeable friend for input. After all, we humans are known for having excellent insights and judgment when it comes to everything—except when it comes to us, and those who are close to us!

1. What kind of greeting does your horse normally give you when you walk into the barn?

2. Does he greet you differently than he does other people? If so, does he greet you more or less enthusiastically than he does others?

3. Is he basically easy to work around? Is he cooperative about grooming, bathing, shoeing, clipping, veterinary care, tacking up, and other routine procedures?

4. When you groom him and tack him up, is he usually quiet and relaxed or does he fuss, squirm, wring his tail, and pin his ears?

5. Does he exhibit any potentially dangerous behaviors, such as nipping or kicking?

6. Does he move forward at your touch, or does he tense and resist?

7. During your riding sessions, is his attitude generally cooperative, or is he inclined to argue with your requests?

8. As he works, are his eyes and ears generally soft and relaxed?

9. How does he react when you introduce something new? Does he take in the new movement or activity calmly? Does he get a little "hot" and excit-ed, perhaps trying too hard? Does he get worried and tense? Does he "shut down" mentally and physically?

10. In your daily work, does he act generally eager and happy to do his job? For instance, if jumping is a large part of your chosen discipline, does he stride confidently to meet the fences, or do you feel as if you have to drive and push him forward? Does he frequently refuse or run out? Or, if you focus on dressage, does he go freely forward with a relaxed, loose stride or does he "suck back" behind the leg, pin his ears when you use your legs or touch him with the whip, habitually grind his teeth or put his tongue out of his mouth, or generally have a sullen or irritated demeanor?

11. To your knowledge, is there abuse or bad handling in his past?

Suitability. Many people tend to think that a horse's talent for a particular equestrian sport equals his suitability to that sport, but this is not necessarily the case. Sure, to do well competitively he needs to have an aptitude for that discipline—jumping ability, movement for dressage, speed for racing, "heart" and bravery for eventing, and so on—but he also needs to *want* to do that activity. I think that suitability is best defined as the right combination of aptitude and attitude for the level at which you want to pursue your chosen discipline.

Many variables color a horse's suitability. For example, a wonderfully kind, willing horse with so-so movement might be a fantastic lower-level dressage horse for a novice rider but would not be suited to a rider whose goal is international-level competition. A "hot," spooky, fabulously talented but difficult-to-handle jumper would probably be a disastrous match for a beginner but could possibly become a star under the right expert rider.

Many horsemen will tell you that they'll take, any day, the horse of average talent who will work his heart out for his rider, over the animal with breathtaking ability but little inherent willingness. My daughter, Jessie, and I once had a prime example of the latter type in our barn. He was incredibly talented for dressage, with outstanding gymnastic ability, conformation, and movement. The work was easy for him. But more often than not, we'd put his bridle on and his ears would go back and his teeth would gnash. We thought, "We'll give him carrots; we'll give him massages; we'll make him happy." We tried every "happy" thing in the book we could think of. Some days, he'd be fine, but on others his ears would go back and his teeth would gnash. You'd put your leg on him when you were riding, and he would kick out and refuse to go forward. To make matters worse, he loved to try to kick his handlers when they turned him out.

Finally, we'd had enough, and we sold him to a woman who was doing lower-level dressage. We later found out that the woman's mother had led the horse out to the paddock—but our dismay soon turned to disbelief when we learned that the horse had ambled along with his nose in her pocket, head down and nuzzling her. His owner takes him jumping; she even dresses him up and takes him in costume classes. He's her pet, and he's a perfect lamb. Why the dramatic change in his personality? Simply that we wanted him in perfect dressage form, and she's happy with him just the way he is. All the pressure is off him, and he's as happy as can be. He's finally found his niche.

1. Make a list of all the activities you do with your horse: dressage, jumping, trail riding, foxhunting, etc. During which activity does he act the happiest?

2. If your horse formerly seemed content with his job but lately has begun acting resistant or careless, consider adjusting the difficulty of the activity to test his "comfort zone." It may be, for example, that he can jump three feet comfortably and confidently but that three feet six is more than he can handle, physically or psychologically. On the other hand, perhaps he's become bored jumping endless tiny fences but would thrive with a bigger challenge (some top show jumpers, for instance, are careless over small fences and don't really get revved up until the rails go up).

3. Try different activities with your horse, and see how he responds. If he's been a dressage horse, like the horse of Jessie's that I described earlier, try taking him over some small fences (get help from a trainer who's knowledgeable in that discipline if the sport is unfamiliar to you). If he's been a show hunter, try some low-level dressage or trail riding. After a few weeks of experimenting with the new activities, go back to your former regimen and gauge his reaction. If he was just bored and in need of a change of scenery, he'll probably approach his work with a renewed zest. But if he truly dislikes the discipline, his attitude will go sour soon after you go back to the activity.

4. Try keeping him in the same discipline, but with a different rider. Not only should your horse be suited to his discipline, but he also should be suited to you. For you and your horse to enjoy a satisfying partnership, his personality and character need to be compatible with your own. It's important to match horse to rider in terms of experience and skill level, to be sure; but it's also important to make sure that horse and rider like each

other and enjoy working together. If you think that you and your horse may not be a good match, try having your instructor or a knowledgeable friend ride him for a week or so. Is he happier with a different rider? Are you even a little bit relieved (even if you don't want to admit it) not to be riding him for a few days?

Set Your Goals

In your journal or notebook, write a sentence or two that describes a realistic goal regarding your horse's willingness. Examples:

"To improve my horse's willingness, I will make sure that my training methods emphasize praise and rewards."

"I will evaluate my horse's willingness as it relates to my chosen discipline, and I will explore different disciplines and levels of difficulty in an effort to determine what job best suits him."

"I will find opportunities to ride some other horses in my chosen sport to give me a comparison to my own horse."

Exercise

Try this small experiment. From a walk, push your horse forward into a trot. The moment he trots, pat him and use your voice to tell him he's a good boy. Repeat this exercise several times. Notice his demeanor. Do his ears go forward? Does he soften in his body? Horses, just like ourselves, enjoy being praised for their work.

Ask yourself: Is your horse more willing to respond to you when you reinforce his actions with praise? If so, do you believe that you can "train" him to be more willing? I'd be willing to bet you can!

Progress Check

Use the following checklist to evaluate your progress in assessing and developing your horse's willingness.

✔ Thirty days after you began emphasizing reinforcement (pats, treats, encouraging words), is there a noticeable change in your horse's demeanor? Have resentful behaviors, such as kicking out at the leg, been replaced with acceptance?

Betsy's Tips

Don't underestimate the importance of evaluating (and working on) your horse's stable manners as you strive to improve his willingness. Try different ways of making the getting-ready-to-work time fun and pleasurable for him—patting, praise, treats, with the emphasis on reinforcement instead of punishment. If resistance is a problem and you can break his cycle of resistance in the barn and get him to think of you as someone whose arrival heralds good things—in other words, that you do more with him than make him work—his attitude toward work may soften. The same positive reinforcement works under saddle as well. Always praise him. Think of the way you'd feel if you worked hard for someone who pushed you and never let you know when you'd done something well. You too would lose your enthusiasm. A little praise can go a long way—for all of us!

✔ Does he greet you more enthusiastically than he did 30 days ago?

✔ Have any of the new activities that you've tried "struck a chord" with your horse? Do you get the feeling that you've discovered what he truly likes to do?

✔ Did decreasing or increasing the difficulty of your daily work produce a change for the better? Do you get the feeling that the problem was that your horse was either overfaced or bored?

✔ Did changing riders produce a change for the better? Do knowledgeable people who know both of you well (such as your instructor) think that you and your horse might be better off with different partners?

ANSWERS TO QUESTIONS ON PAGE 64

1. Because the seat is the center or core of the rider's strength and balance and therefore is the main source of influence over the horse.
2. To maintain the horse's rhythm, activity, energy, and balance during the transitions.
3. (a) As part of the seat, in initiating and finishing aids, and (b) To help bring the forward energy up so that the horse takes a springier, loftier step.
4. Because the horse must be positioned correctly during suppling exercises, and because the aids maintain the proper rhythm and tempo that are prerequisites to suppleness and relaxation.
5. To receive the energy created by the seat and legs and to complete the "circle of the aids."

4.1
CONTACT *is established by the communication between horse and rider. The horse moves forward from his haunches into, and "accepts," the rider's hands.*

CHAPTER FOUR

Building Block 3: *Contact*

Contact (kon′takt), *n.*
1. the act or state of touching; a touching or meeting, as of two things, people, etc. 2. a condition in which two or more individuals or groups are placed in communication with each other.

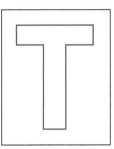

he German National Equestrian Federation explains the concept of contact as follows:

Contact is a soft and steady connection between the rider's hand and the horse's mouth. While training progresses, the horse should be ridden from behind into the elastically yielding hand. The contact will then be even on both reins when riding straight ahead, and a little stronger on the outside rein when riding on a circle.

To achieve a contact the reins may not be moved backwards. Contact has to be the result of well-developed propulsive power. When forward driving aids are applied the horse has to move forward into the contact.

…Contact does not mean that the horse may lie on the rider's hand. He must find his own balance and not try to use the reins as a "fifth leg."

…To establish a contact the rider must bring the horse's hind legs further underneath his body. This stretches and elasticates [sic] the neck and back muscles.…Through this swinging back the propulsive force generated by the quarters can now be transmitted forward to the horse's mouth. The horse submits to the energy coming from behind: he flexes in the poll and champs the bit—in other words he is on the bit.[1]

1 *USDF Manual*, pp. 167-168. Excerpted from *Principles of Riding: The Official Handbook of the German National Equestrian Federation*; reprinted with permission of Half Halt Press.

The MIND Element: Connection

What You Need to Know

Despite these and other explanations in dressage texts, the concept of contact is often misunderstood by riders who think that "taking contact" means kicking with their legs and pulling or holding with the reins. Contact is not something that is "done to" a horse with the reins and the bit. It can be initiated, asked of, or coaxed from—but not done to—the horse. Shortening or taking a stronger hold of your reins is not the same as achieving contact. Rather, contact is an agreeable, dynamic communication initiated by the rider and sought and established by the horse, who steps forward with energy and flows into the rider's hands.

Contact is a vast concept—perhaps the most broad and wide-ranging of all the components of the *Training Pyramid*. For all practical purposes, contact is the foundation of the upper-level work because it is the point at which the rider establishes a physical and psychological *connection* with the horse. Establishing that connection can be elusive and difficult, and for those reasons many riders find it challenging at this stage of training. Happily, though, those who do master the concept of contact usually are able to advance quite a bit further up the ladder of training.

As you may have noticed when you read the German Federation's explanation of contact, dressage texts tend to discuss contact only in terms of what the horse does physically. But contact involves so much more than physical skill. First, of course, you have to understand what connection in the horse is. Then, to appreciate the concept of connection in the horse, you have to understand what it means to be connected in your own body—the ability to keep your "form" or position, no matter what. Finally, you have to understand the various types of connections between horse and rider.

Establishing contact is much like establishing trust. You can't force someone to trust you; nor can you earn someone's trust instantaneously. Likewise, you cannot give a certain set of aids or perform some specific maneuver and instantly achieve true contact with your horse. There are many layers or depths to each phase of the *Training Pyramid*. The first step is to understand clearly that *you* are the tool and means of communication with your horse to connect his body and yours so that they blend and work together as one harmonious partnership.

When a horse accepts the rein contact by flexing at the poll and softening his jaw, he is said to be on the bit. When he not only accepts the contact but moves into it by pushing forward from behind, coordinating and engaging his entire body, he begins to become what we call connected or "through." Your aids begin to act on his body in a cyclical fashion. Sitting deep in the saddle and using your leg aids cause him to step further underneath himself and to use the joints of his hindquarters as springs that flex and release energy forward and upward. That energy travels forward, over flexed and activated back muscles, the crest of the neck, and the poll into the jaw, where it meets the rein contact and as a result is channeled back to the hindquarters via the abdominal muscles, which serve to lift the back as they activate. This process of creating, recycling, and renewing energy is known as the "circle of the aids" or the "muscle ring." When a horse is thus connected, the rider can actually influence his hindquarters by using half-halts and balancing into the reins!

In essence, every part of the connected horse's body is in balance with every other part, and he is using all of his muscles and joints together in a harmonious fashion. But before you can achieve this state of "throughness," you must be equally in tune with your own body and able to use it in the same coordinated, whole-body way. Your body is your tool for communication with your horse. In Chapters Two and Three, I discussed the importance of strength and flexibility in achieving rhythm and suppleness. To achieve contact, you have to take these attributes one step further: You need to coordinate them, and to learn by *engaging your core,* so that you remain stable even when making a movement with one part of your body (e.g., when changing the positioning of your legs to ask for a flying change). In other words, you must find your own physical connection.

As I mentioned earlier, contact requires that you learn to connect—physically and mentally—with your horse. After all, "to make contact" means to communicate, and that's exactly the purpose that contact serves while you're riding. So the final step in establishing contact with your horse is to learn how to use your body to influence his body—to activate his muscles and his mind in a way that will bring him into balance and unity with you. It is at this point that you and your horse will begin to become one.

Assess Your Understanding

Take the following quiz to assess your understanding of the concept of contact. Compare your responses with the answers on page 141, and give yourself one point for every correct answer.

1. What must you have before contact can be attained?

2. What is the first step in seeking contact?

   Shorten the reins

   Send the horse forward from the leg

   Do a transition

3. In what primary way does rein contact help make a horse "through"?

   Stops him from running away

   Helps the rider keep her position

   Causes the forward energy to "recycle" back to the hindquarters

Set Your Goals

In your journal or notebook, write a sentence or two that describes a realistic goal (remember, "realistic" means that it's achievable in 30 days or less) regarding your understanding of contact. Example:

"I will learn to tell the difference between a horse that accepts the contact and one that's being 'pulled together' in front and not truly pushing into the contact from behind."

Exercises and Progress Check

EXERCISE 1: Video Review

Have someone videotape your ride as you work on improving contact. Study the videotape and notice when your horse is really on contact: soft in the hands but keeping a connection through his body and yours. Notice when he loses the connection. Establish visual images of both situations in your mind, and at the same time try to recall the way that each felt as you were riding.

4.2

4.3

a. *Evading the contact by going above the bit.*

b. *A giving hand and a balanced horse. The horse's legs are underneath and supporting the body, the haunches are active, the shoulder is free, and there is a comfortable balance in the neck and reins without the rider's pulling on the reins.*

c. *Evading the contact by going behind the bit.*

d. *Horse being ridden "front to back," with the rider's hands forcing the "contact."*

e. *Good acceptance of contact.*

EXERCISE 2: Train Your Eye

Watching horses go, either in person or on videotape, is one of the best ways to teach yourself to recognize the differences between true "throughness" (acceptance of contact); incorrect "front-to-back" riding, in which the rider tries to force the horse to take the contact by holding with the reins; and the various evasions that horses use to avoid the contact, such as going above or behind the bit or backing off the contact by "sucking back" behind the leg. To get you started, I asked Jessie to demonstrate proper acceptance of contact as well as the common flaws. Take a look at the series of photos below, and see if you can match each photo with the correct description.

4.4

4.5

4.6

(Stumped? Turn to page 141 for the correct answers.)

Were you able to match each photo to the correct caption? If so, congratulations! You've learned how to assess a horse's acceptance of contact by looking at his outline and frame. If you missed one or more, carefully compare the "incorrect" photos with the photo that depicts good contact.

Now it's time to watch some horses go and see if you can discern between correct and incorrect contact. Keep in mind that even the most experienced and well-trained horse may show moments in which he is not fully connected and accepting the contact. This is simply because movement is ever-changing and needs constant adjustment to remain in balance. For the most part, however, the contact should remain soft, steady, and elastic.

Betsy's Tips

In most cases, contact should remain steadiest with the outside rein (the rein opposite the side to which the horse is bent or is traveling). That's because the outside rein acts as a gentle wall to keep the horse's shoulders on the line of travel, preventing the outside shoulder from dropping to the outside. When you look at photos or watch horses go, you will occasionally see the rider's inside rein slacken. A momentarily slack inside rein does not necessarily mean that the rider has lost the contact; if the horse remains soft and does not alter his frame, he is actually demonstrating his acceptance of the outside-rein contact. Dressage tests even require that riders slacken the inside rein as a test of their mounts' accepting the outside rein. When both hands give in a forward direction, toward the horse's mouth, the exercise is known by the German word *überstreichen* (fig. 4.7).

4.7

Jessie tests Magdalena's acceptance of the outside rein by momentarily slackening her inside rein in the canter. The mare maintains her rhythm, tempo, roundness, and bend—a lovely picture.

The BODY Element: Coordination

What You Need to Have

Some people hear the word *coordination* and assume that the term refers to *hand-eye coordination,* which is the skill needed to do things like hit a golf ball or play a musical instrument. Hand-eye coordination is an important element in riding, but riding requires an even broader type of coordination: *body coordination,* which is the combination of balance, flexibility, control, dexterity, and—very important— "feeling" or sensitivity toward your horse's body and movements.

Body coordination is important because, if you cannot coordinate your own body, it will be very difficult—if not impossible—for you to honestly coordinate your horse's body. After all, it is because of your coordination that your horse learns how to organize and balance his own body (or not!), which he must do to be able to accept contact. A rider who lacks coordination may hang onto the reins for balance, grip with her legs, collapse in her waist, or give her horse random and conflicting signals. In turn, rather than being coaxed into a conversation of balance and energy, the horse answers his rider's most dominant body signal or, worse, "tunes out" or tenses and resists out of confusion or discomfort because the messages he's receiving are jumbled, unclear, or loud. But when you ride with sensitivity, balance, and deliberation, you will gain your horse's attention—and, eventually, his trust. (Sensitivity consists of listening for your horse's answers to the questions that you ask him.) When that happens, he will stretch into contact with you. Keep in mind that it is easier for him to obey a single message from you than it is for him to react to four or five issued simultaneously.

Some people think that coordination is inherent—an innate trait that you either have or you don't. But coordination while riding is not a gift; it has more to do with being able to move each part of your body wherever you need to, the instant you need to and in harmony with the rest of your body, all while in a constantly changing environment. Fortunately, this kind of body coordination can be learned.

Assess Your Skill Level

Stand in front of a full-length mirror. Put a sturdy book under the ball of each foot so that your heels are down (two dictionaries would be ideal). Bend your knees so that you're standing in riding position, and bounce softly in the rhythm and tempo of your horse's trot. (If you're having trouble recalling the tempo while you're unmounted, try putting on the trot music you found on page 30.) Hold your hands and arms in riding position. Take one hand out to the side and bring it back in as you bounce. Try it with the other hand. Now twist your upper body to one side and then the other as you bounce. Can you maintain the trot rhythm and tempo and keep everything else in your body the same as you isolate the movements of your arm and torso? If not, you'll benefit from some work on your body coordination.

Set Your Goals

In your journal or notebook, write a sentence or two that describes a realistic goal regarding body coordination. Examples:

"I will take longe lessons to learn how to use my seat and legs independent of my hands."

"I will ride without stirrups for ten minutes a day until I develop the strength and body control to keep my legs quietly against my horse's sides without accidentally bumping or kicking him."

Exercises

Core stability is an essential element of coordination. Along with attaining axial elongation and functional strength, you need to be able to tilt (or straighten) your pelvis as necessary to achieve many goals in riding, including the driving aids, half-halting, turns and lateral work, and more.

The basic position is the neutral pelvis. This is the ideal position while weight-bearing (such as when you are standing), for you can "tap into" your core muscles much more easily. Maintain a neutral pelvic position as you learn any new *Pilates* exercise (figs. 4.8 A & B). When you feel comfortable engaging your core muscles during an exercise, try the exercise with a posterior pelvic tilt—which is the correct pelvic position for riding (figs. 4.9 A & B).

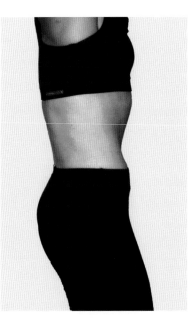

4.8 A & B
Neutral Pelvis

Susan's hip bones are level with her pubic bone, there is just a slight arch in her lower back, and her abdominal muscles are engaged. This pelvic position is ideal for strengthening your core in Pilates, for power with your seat in riding. The ideal pelvic position is posterior (A).

Standing view of neutral pelvis (B).

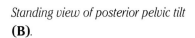

4.9 A & B
Posterior Pelvic Tilt

Susan has tipped her imaginary compass north, flattening her back against the floor. Although the directions for this exercise specify placing your hands on your hips, Susan has extended her arms over her head to give a better view of her lower back and pelvic position (A).

Standing view of posterior pelvic tilt (B).

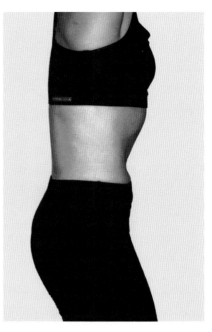

4.10 A & B
Anterior Pelvic Tilt
Susan has tipped her imaginary compass south, arching her lower back off the floor and pointing her tailbone down toward the floor **(A)**.

Standing view of anterior pelvic tilt **(B)**.

EXERCISE 1: Compass Tilts

To learn to feel the *neutral-pelvis* position, lie on the floor on your back with your knees bent. Place your hands on your hips. Pretend that you have a compass on your abdomen, with north being toward your head and south being toward your knees. Tip your compass first north and then south several times until you feel comfortable with the pelvic movement.

Next, try to achieve the same "north and south" pelvic movements by using only your *core* abdominal muscles and not your gluteal (buttocks) muscles. Don't be surprised if this is more difficult and produces less pelvic movement. Think of "zipping up" your abdominals and quieting down your "glutes."

Notice that, when you tip your compass north, your back flattens against the floor; and, when you tip your compass south, your lower back arches. To find your neutral pelvis, tip your compass south, aiming your tailbone down toward the floor. Your pelvis is now in what is called an anterior pelvic tilt, and you'll notice that your lower back is arched (figs. 4.10 A & B). This is the exact *opposite* of the desired pelvic position in riding!

While keeping your tailbone pointed down, reduce or soften the lower-back arch by drawing in your abdominals. Do not flatten the curve so much that your back is flat against the floor. Check to ensure that your core is engaged and taut under your fingers. If your pelvis is in neutral position, the tops of your hip bones should be level with your pubic bone. This is the position that you want to maintain during most of the *Pilates* movements. After you feel confident attaining and maintaining a neutral pelvis, try the *Pilates* movements with your compass tipped north, which creates a *posterior pelvic tilt*—the correct angle for riding.

EXERCISE 2: Unmounted Coordination Tests

Loop a piece of stretch tubing (available from fitness-supply stores and catalogs) around a sturdy post or pole. Hold the ends of the tubing at elbow height, as if they are reins. Stand with your legs at hip's width and bend your hip, knee, and ankle joints as if you are sitting in the saddle. Begin bouncing lightly as if you are sitting the trot. As you bounce, extend one arm out to the side and then return it to starting position. Do the same with the other arm. Then try pulling one arm across your body and returning it to starting position; switch arms and repeat. Can you maintain your riding position and the tempo and rhythm of your bouncing while you coordinate the arm movements?

For a variation of this exercise, you'll need a helper. Sit on an exercise ball, facing your helper. Hold the ends of a piece of stretch tubing as described above, and have your helper hold the loop. Bounce on the ball in riding rhythm and try the arm movements as described above. How is your coordination this time?

Progress Check

Use the following checklist to assess your progress in improving your body coordination. During the 30 days that you're working toward the goal that you expressed in *Set Your Goals* on page 116, refer to this list once every week or so and see which items you can check off. After you've checked them all off, congratulations! You've demonstrated considerable improvement in your body coordination.

- ✔ Were you able to stay focused and balanced in your "core" as you practiced controlling your pelvic position (p. 118).
- ✔ Can you find the same balanced position in the saddle and stay centered in your "core"?
- ✔ When you're riding, do you focus your attention on working from your "core" and on "pulling your belly button toward your spine"?

✔ Can you hold that "core" position in the saddle without gripping upward with your legs?

✔ Can you keep your upper body erect and positioned over your horse's center of gravity as he moves without using the reins to support your upper body?

✔ Can you keep your legs resting against your horse's sides except for when you want to use them to give an aid?

✔ Can you give an aid with one leg or hand without automatically using the other?

Betsy's Tips

Much dressage work above the lowest levels requires a great deal of body coordination on the part of the rider. The aids for many movements require dead-on accurate timing, the ability to stay centered and grounded in your "core," the synchronized use of your entire body, and the ability to make rapid-fire changes in your body positioning. And here's the trick: It should look as if you're doing nothing! Giving the aids at this level demands complete body coordination as well as a finely tuned sense of timing and quick reflexes.

Achieving success at the highest level of dressage takes a tremendous amount of hard work, resources, and the luck of having the right horse as your partner—and talent most certainly helps. Yet some riders get discouraged if they're not realizing that kind of success and frustrate themselves by yearning for something that simply may not be possible for them, at least at this point in time—or, worse, by buying a high-powered horse that they don't have the skills or experience to handle and getting scared or hurt, blaming the horse for not staying at this level for the sake of the rider, or quitting riding altogether.

I urge you to evaluate your interests, skills, abilities, experience, and goals *realistically* and to strive to "be all that you can be" given your own unique set of circumstances: your time, your resources, your lifestyle, your other interests and commitments, and your goals for your riding.

The SPIRIT Element: Consistency and Steadiness

What You Need to Be

As I've explained, getting your horse to reach into the rein contact requires trust. He must trust that you will remain in balance with him and that you will not accidentally bump his sides with your legs or his mouth with your hands. But he must also learn to trust in you; and that means trusting that you will treat him kindly and fairly, understanding that you may push him but knowing that you will not ask him for anything that is beyond his ability, and that you will not surprise him by altering your training methods. Your approach remains consistent: Every day, you repeat the same lessons and give the aids in the same way. And your attitude remains consistent: You're not overly permissive one day and overly critical the next, and you don't allow outside worries or other factors to color the way that you treat him. When you train with consistency and steadiness, he will come to rely on you to be true to your "word."

Horses, like all animals, learn through repetition. In addition, horses thrive on routine: being fed, turned out, and ridden at the same time each day. Within the routine of their daily schedules, horses gain confidence by being worked in a systematic fashion. This is not to suggest that you should drill your horse until he rebels from sheer boredom; most horses enjoy some variety in their work, such as regular trail riding. However, within your training sessions he will make the most progress and gain the most confidence if you are consistent in your requests and steady in your attitude. If he does not know what to expect from you and isn't sure what you want from him, he will not make progress because he'll always be trying to figure out what you want. You would not expect a child to learn multiplication by going out for recess one day, singing class the next day, and never showing up for a math class! Horses, like children, learn through repetition and consistency.

Again, I am not suggesting that you ride like an automaton or that you drill the same handful of exercises, day in and day out. A good rider adjusts her program accordingly to suit her horse's physical and mental states on that day. For example, one day, he may need to be ridden very forward; the next, he may benefit from an emphasis on suppling exercises. And you may find that you need to be stronger in your seat one day and softer the next, depending on his mood. The important thing is that the work remains consistent within the framework of the *Training Pyramid*—that the basics are established and strengthened in the same systematic manner—and that you strive to adhere to a certain set of consistent standards in your training sessions. For instance, it does your horse no good to allow him to make crooked, sloppy halts for four days in a row and then to get after him for not halting square on the fifth. That's not his fault; it's yours.

Just as your training program should be consistent, so should your attitude be one of steadiness. You are patient, calm, and relaxed, with your goals firmly in mind, no matter what he does. You're not easily distracted or rattled, and—ideally—you ride the same way whether you're at home or at a show. It naturally follows that the same principles apply as you work around him in the stable.

Assess Your Psyche

How consistent and steady are you as a rider and trainer? Take the following short quiz to assess yourself. For each example, circle the letter that represents the response that is most like the way you usually behave.

1. Before I get on my horse, I usually:
   a) Don't really have anything in mind. I get on and take it from there
   b) Mentally review my previous session and decide what steps I'll take to build on that today
   c) Just want to escape the pressures of the day

2. If my horse acts resistant during a session, I tend to:
   a) Get irritated and smack him with the whip
   b) Try to figure out what's causing the resistance and develop a strategy for working through it
   c) Get off; I don't want to fight with him

3. The week before a show, I'm likely to:
   a) Panic—I've done little or nothing to prepare
   b) Systematically continue working on the same things I've been working on all along
   c) Slack off in my training. I'm so nervous, I'd rather not ride at all

4. In clinics or lessons, instructors tend to:
   a) Advise me to back off and work on strengthening my horse's basics
   b) Give me exercises and techniques to help improve my horse's weaknesses
   c) Get after me for not demanding enough of myself and my horse in daily training

5. If I'm in a bad mood before my ride, I usually:
   a) Struggle (not always successfully) not to take my frustrations out on my horse
   b) Put the events of the day out of my mind for the duration of the ride by focusing on my horse
   c) Decide not to ride that day. I can't trust myself not to take my emotions out on my horse

If you had mostly "a" responses, you may find it difficult to maintain consistency because you don't plan ahead; you're reactive instead of proactive. Because you find yourself "putting out fires," you may tend to get defensive, which encourages your horse to do the same.

If you had mostly "b" responses, you plan ahead and strive to maintain a positive, focused approach to your training and riding.

If you had mostly "c" responses, you tend to react to potentially stressful or challenging situations by avoiding them, instead of by learning how to deal with them and turn them into positives.

Set Your Goals

In your journal or notebook, write a sentence or two that describes a realistic goal regarding consistency and steadiness. Use your score from the above quiz to guide you. Examples:

"I will take a more proactive, leadership approach to my training sessions."

"I will learn coping strategies so that I can deal successfully with issues and problems."

Exercises

EXERCISE 1: Start Small

Use your own athletic workouts as your guide to building consistency in your training with your horse. Concentrate on stabilizing your core, think of stabilizing his core, and let everything flow from there. Repeat and stay steady. Now go for a bit more.

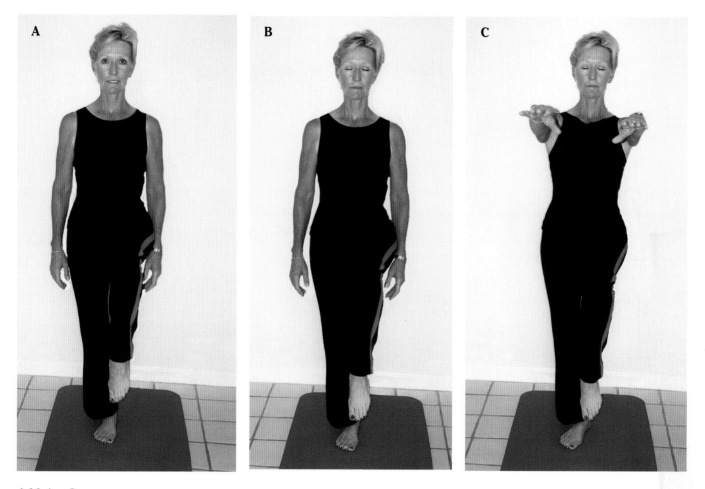

4.11 A – C
Balance Check
Can you lift one leg as I'm doing here, and maintain your postural alignment? **(A)**.

What about with your eyes closed **(B)**.

Challenge yourself by trying different positions. Here, I'm balancing on one leg, arms extended and eyes closed. When you close your eyes, "tune in" to which parts of your body get most wobbly. Can you center yourself and regain your balance? **(C)**.

EXERCISE 2: Balance Check
Improve your balance and coordination (figs. 4.11 A – C).

EXERCISE 3: Mounted Exercise
Establish a 20-meter circle in a rhythmic, relaxed walk. Ask for a transition to the trot by sitting up straight, letting your weight drop down through your spine into the back of your seat, "scooping" your seat bones forward, closing and supporting with your upper legs against the saddle, and giving a "tap" with your lower legs. Allow your horse to move with active haunches forward into your hands. Trot for only eight to ten steps, and make a transition back to walk. Repeat the sequence, focusing on maintaining consistency and steadiness in your body until he becomes consistent and steady in his response to you. The goal of this exercise is first to develop the consistency in your own body, and then to become aware of how he follows your consistency.

EXERCISE 4: Write It Down

Are you as consistent in your riding and training methods as you think you are? By writing down and reviewing your notes on previous sessions, you'll become a more thoughtful and proactive (instead of reactive) rider. You'll also be able to do some "lesson planning."

EXERCISE 5: Raise the Bar

It's tempting to get lax in one's riding, especially if there's no instructor around to see it! Make an effort to challenge yourself and to keep your standards high. Focus on quality, not quantity. Make a few truly round circles instead of endless egg-shaped ones. Don't settle for sloppy halts: Square up every halt, every time. Don't cut your corners: Make yourself really ride through them in a balanced manner. Take longe lessons to improve your position. Audit (or watch videos of) clinics with top trainers. Watching the best in action gives you a picture in your mind's eye and something to strive for, and also gives you patterns of success to emulate.

Progress Check

Use the following checklist to evaluate your progress toward your goal regarding consistency and steadiness.

- ✔ Before each ride, could you explain to your trainer or a friend what you worked on the last time, how that session ended, and how you plan to approach today's ride?
- ✔ Do you feel more prepared for your next show or clinic?
- ✔ If your horse resists or misbehaves, can you "count to ten" as you evaluate the problem instead of simply feeling frustrated?
- ✔ Can you be positive and relaxed around your horse, even if you've had a bad day?
- ✔ As you gained steadiness in your own body, did you notice the way that your horse reflected what you'd accomplished?

Betsy's Tips

Practice being consistent in everything you do with your horse, from feeding and grooming to riding. Try to incorporate these qualities into your daily life. Make it a habit to check yourself to see if you are reacting to things around you, even outside your riding, with consistency and steadiness.

HORSE
contact AND THE HORSE

The MIND Element: Forward Within a Connection

What Your Horse Needs to Know

Contact organizes the horse's body, assembling all of his body parts to move forward and fluidly. As I've explained, a horse that's "through" or "connected" allows the energy of his hindquarters to flow forward, over his topline and arched neck, into his softly chewing jaw, and then back via his abdominal muscles to his hindquarters, where the circle of the aids is renewed.

At this stage of training, the horse must understand and accept a concept that is crucial to his advancement: that *he must go forward into and in acceptance of the contact*. If he does not grasp the concept, or if he does not fully accept it, his rider will inevitably have problems when she tries to move on in her training. The horse must allow himself to be steadily pushed into a contact that contains and channels his forward energy. He must accept being "held" between the rider's legs and hands like a strung bow. He must learn that he is not to back off from the contact, or to lean on it, or to run through it; he must allow it to help shape his body and conduct his energy. He needs to understand that he is not simultaneously being told "go" and "whoa," but that he must balance his body. Consider what he must be thinking and feeling. Try to put yourself "in his shoes" as you teach him the concepts of moving forward from the leg and accepting the feeling of contact into the bit.

Assess Your Horse's Understanding

Evaluate your horse's understanding and acceptance of the concept of going forward into the contact by considering the following statements:

When I attempt to push my horse into the contact, he typically:

1. Slows down, raises his head and neck, or goes behind the vertical.

2. Lifts his back and arches his neck as he takes a more powerful (but still rhythmic) step with his hind legs.

3. Leans on my hands.

4. Tries to run through my hands.

If you chose 1, 3, or 4, you need to ask yourself why your horse does those things. What could be the reason that he does not fully comprehend (or accept) that he must go forward into the contact?

Set Your Goals

In your journal or notebook, write a sentence or two that describes a realistic goal regarding your horse's understanding of going forward within the connection. Examples:

"In 30 days, I will find the way to help my horse understand how to maintain his forward impulsion, rhythm, and tempo while on contact."

"I'd like for my horse to understand that he must move *into* the contact—that he isn't allowed to use it as a 'fifth leg' or to run through it entirely."

Exercises

EXERCISE 1: Encouraging Contact

If your horse backs off the contact or "hides" behind the bit, keep your hands still and push him forward from a driving seat toward a steady and quiet hand while making many transitions between gaits and between paces within a gait. Trying to "fix" this problem by using your hands will only aggravate the problem. Always search for an answer by going in a more forward tempo.

EXERCISE 2: Engaging the Hind Legs

If your horse tends to lean on your hands instead of allowing his hind legs to be pushed up underneath him, the following exercises should prove helpful: trot-halt-trot and walk-halt-walk transitions, leg-yield, shoulder-in, frequent changes of direction, and positioning him with a slight counterflexion to soften his outside jaw.

EXERCISE 3: Respecting the Hands

If your horse tends to run through your hands, halt quietly as soon as he quickens. In the halt, flex him softly in one direction and then the other as you coax him to soften his jaw. Then, if he accepts the bit, ask for a couple of steps of reinback. Repeat the sequence every time he tries to run through your hands. If, however, he offers reinback on his own when you halt instead of waiting for your aids, go for-

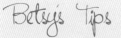

Betsy's Tips

If you are having real difficulties with contact, ask a reputable professional to get on your horse to explain to him exactly what you want. You will spare your horse and yourself a lot of frustration. Learn by watching the professional carefully and get a clear picture in your mind of what he or she did; ask for a clear verbal explanation as well. Keeping the picture and the description in mind, repeat the work yourself. Sometimes "seeing it" is believing it!

ward immediately. If he gets strong in the bridle again, halt without reining back for a few times until he stops anticipating. Use your intuition and common sense as to which transition to use while doing this work.

Progress Check

Use the following checklist to assess your horse's progress in learning that he must go forward within the connection.

✔ If you have mirrors in your riding arena, watch your horse's outline. If his tendency is to go behind the vertical when he feels the contact, is his profile closer to vertical or slightly in front of the vertical? If he "curls up" with his neck, is his poll now the highest point? If you don't have access to mirrors, have someone videotape your ride or ask a knowledgeable helper to watch your horse go.

✔ If your horse likes to lean on the bit and "trail" his haunches out behind, is he lighter in the hand without going behind the vertical? Does he give you more of a feeling of compactness—no more "head in one county and hindquarters in another"? Under your seat, can you feel the thrust of his hind legs as they cause his back to lift and swing?

✔ If your horse tends to panic within the connection and quicken to try to escape, is he more relaxed moving into the contact and better able to maintain a rhythm and tempo? Can you use your leg to encourage him to take a more powerful step with his hind legs without his speeding up?

✔ Do the reins feel elastic in your hands, as if a big rubber band is connecting your hands to your horse's mouth? If they feel tight and "dead," you may be gripping or he may be leaning, causing a tug of war. If they feel consistently light, with little more than the weight of the reins in your hands, he may be behind the bit (momentary lightness, especially on the inside rein, is okay, as long as you're sure that you can move him "into" the reins).

✔ *The ultimate progress check: the "stretching circle."* Develop a 20-meter circle in a rhythmic working trot rising. When you feel that your horse is moving well into the contact, allow both hands to gradually move forward toward his mouth; don't change anything else. If he truly accepts the contact, he will stretch his head and neck out and down, "following" the contact into your hands yet continuing to move in rhythm and balance. After he

has made one circle while stretching down, see if you can gradually pick up the reins and return to the working trot without his changing his tempo, rhythm, relaxation, or acceptance of the contact. If he will "chew the reins out of your hands" like this in both directions, you've done it! He's demonstrated excellent connection and willingness to go forward into the contact—and you've just done an important movement from the Training and First Level dressage tests (fig. 4.12).

The BODY Element: Balance

What Your Horse Needs to Have

Among the several dictionary definitions of the word *balance* are "a state of equilibrium, as among weights or forces" and "a state of stability, as of the body or the emotions." Those definitions describe exactly what your horse needs to develop at this stage of his training: equilibrium in his muscular strength and flexibility, and stability in his entire frame. As you now know, a horse that is connected and accepting of the rein contact has activated the synergy of his muscle ring, and all of the muscles of his body are working in a harmonious and cyclical fashion. For the muscle ring to function correctly and efficiently, all of the muscles must be well developed, with no single group of muscles over- or underdeveloped. He must be balanced longitudinally, so that he remains aligned from his tail to his nose and does not fall onto his forehand; and he must be balanced laterally, so that he travels straight and is equally flexible in both directions. His muscles must support one another, just as your muscles must support one another. Finally, he must be able to maintain his balance in all three gaits while traveling on a straight line, in turns and circles, in lateral movements, and during transitions.

Assess Your Horse's Skill Level

How balanced is your horse? Take the following quiz to find out.

1. Repeat the "stretching circle" exercise from page 128. Does your horse's rhythm or tempo change? If he speeds up when you give the reins, he may have fallen onto his forehand and is trying to "catch up" with his displaced center of gravity.

2. Do you have difficulty riding deeply into your corners or making accurate turns onto the center line of the arena? If your horse habitually tries to cut his corners or swings wide on turns down the center line, he may be having trouble balancing his body in the tighter turns. Check, too, to make sure that your position is correct and that you are using your inside leg into your outside rein correctly, to help him balance in corners.

3. When you ride a straight line, does your horse tend to drift one way or the other? Insufficient balance may be part of the problem.

Set Your Goals

In your journal or notebook, write a sentence or two that describes a realistic goal regarding your horse's balance. Examples:

"In the next 30 days, I will be able to hold my position and give the aids well enough to balance my horse so that I can ride deeper corners in both directions."

"I will be able to do the stretching-circle (*überstreichen*) exercise without my horse's speeding up and falling onto his forehand by having him focus on the use of my seat and upper leg."

Exercises

The following exercises are useful in teaching your horse to balance himself.

EXERCISE 1: The Four-Point Halt

Begin by walking on a 20-meter circle at A. Circle a few times; then, when your horse is walking in a steady rhythm and tempo, halt at A. Walk forward and halt again on the center line at the point on the circle that's across from A (near L). Repeat until your horse is walking and halting at the two points calmly and accurately, and then add the other two "halt points" where the 20-meter circle touches the track. Make sure that the circle geometry remains accurate throughout (figs. 4.13 A – C). Next, repeat the sequence (first two-point halt, then four-point halt) in trot (figs. 4.14 A – C and 4.15 A – C).

Soon, your horse will begin to anticipate halting at each point. Take advantage of that anticipation by introducing half-halts instead of full halts: Push him forward back into the trot as he begins to halt. Alternate the four points on the circle with half-halts and full halts. If you feel him beginning to fall behind your leg or to lose his forward impulsion, go forward, even if you need to leave the circle and refresh him with an energetic rising trot down the long side of the arena. Then return to the circle and repeat the exercise (figs. 4.16 A & B). After he has mastered the exercise in the trot, try it in the canter. Begin with the two-point halt. When he's comfortable doing that in the canter, go to the four-point halt. Then try doing a half-halt instead of a full halt at every other point on the four-point circle.

Next, increase the difficulty of the exercise by using the leg-yielding exercise from Chapter Three (p. 90). Starting on a 20-meter circle, leg-yield in to a 15-meter circle. Straighten your horse, begin to leg-yield out on the circle, and ask him to canter. Canter around on the circle and walk when you reach A, and then leg-yield in at the walk for a few strides until you reach point two (between K and V). Leg-yield out to point three (near L) and pick up the canter. The leg-yielding is not dramatic—just a couple of strides—it's more of a loosening and suppling of his body than his feet coming in and going out. Canter once around the full circle and repeat the exercise. Reverse and repeat the exercise in the opposite direction.

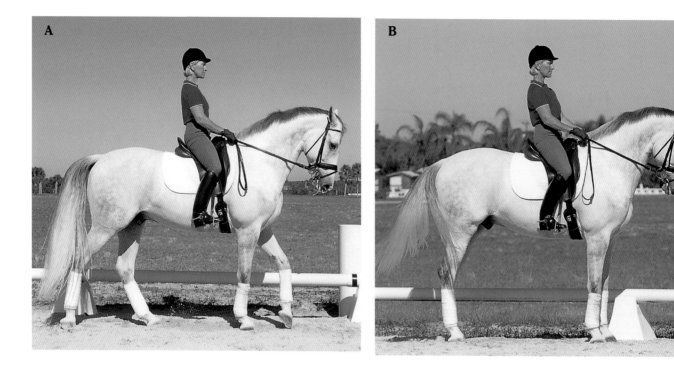

4.13 A – C
The Four-Point Halt

Manhattan shows a good example of walk-to-halt-to-walk transitions for the four-point halt exercise. He has an energetic walk from behind, moving nicely into my hand **(A)**.

He is obedient to my seat aids as he takes his final step to a square halt **(B)**.

His energy is forward and into my hands through contact with the reins as he obediently walks forward **(C)**.

4.14 A – C
Trot-Halt Transition

Here is Heraut, an upper-level, more developed horse in a balanced lovely trot **(A)**.

There is an increase in the activity in the hind end as I use my core strength to hold my position to influence the halt through my lower back **(B)**.

Heraut settles into what will be a balanced halt **(C)**.

4.15 A – C
Halt to Trot
Halt **(A)**.

Moving to trot **(B)**...

... still using the influence of the driving seat in the second or third stride out of halt **(C)**.

4.16 A & B
Magdalena has begun to anticipate the halt **(A)**...

...so, the next time, instead of halting, Jessie introduces half-halts by pushing Magdalena back into the trot as soon as the mare begins to halt **(B)**.

4.17 A & B
Trot-Canter Transition

Trot-canter transitions on the circle are an excellent way of asking your horse to come into balance and to accept a good contact. Manhattan is at the moment of his first step from trot into canter and demonstrates the carrying power in his haunches and lightness in the forehand **(A)**.

In the second and third stride his whole body comes into balance **(B)**.

EXERCISE 2: Trot-Canter Transitions

Another good way to get your horse to come into balance and to accept a good contact is through the use of the trot-canter transitions that you learned in Chapter Three (p. 92), now increasing the difficulty. Begin on a 20-meter circle on the right rein in the trot, with a slight counter-flexion. At A, leg-yield inward for just a few strides. Straighten him and then flex him to the right. Once you have a nice inward bend, leg-yield back out to the 20-meter circle; as you leg-yield out, ask for the canter. Remember, doing the canter transition through the leg-yield will bring his inside hind leg nicely underneath himself as he connects solidly into both reins. Now discipline yourself to do the transition on two points of the circle. Remember the feeling of the leg-yield at each point; but instead of physically pushing his entire body over, just bend him around your inside leg and ask for a transition into either trot or canter. Repeat the sequence until you feel he's done it sufficiently. Change rein and repeat the exercise (figs. 4.17 A & B).

B

Betsy's Tips

Keep in mind that active working haunches are the source of your horse's ability to balance.

Progress Check

Retake the horse-assessment exercises on page 130. The following items are good indicators of progress:

✔ Your horse can do the "stretching circle" exercise in both directions while maintaining his rhythm, tempo, and longitudinal balance.

✔ You can ride 25 percent (or more) more deeply into your corners in both directions.

✔ You can make a smooth and accurate turn down the center line without losing rhythm, tempo, or the rein contact.

The SPIRIT Element: Trust and Confidence

What Your Horse Needs to Be

All good relationships are based on trust—a mutual faith that the other will act with integrity, honesty, and good will. From trust springs confidence, which is a feeling of reassurance based on the combination of trust and positive past experiences.

In riding terms, trust means that your horse believes that you will not frighten or hurt him, that you will always be there to care for him, and that you will never ask him to do something that is dangerous or beyond his capability. A confident horse not only trusts his rider but also trusts himself. He believes that he can do what is asked of him, and he understands what his job is.

Once violated, trust is extremely difficult to regain. If your horse was mistreated or handled poorly by a previous owner or trainer, he may have developed fears or phobias that certain circumstances will always trigger, even if you ride him expertly and never lift a hand to him. He may have learned to fear or even resent humans. Biting, kicking, rearing, and other vices all can be learned behaviors that stem from provocation or self-defense. Fortunately, truly dangerous horses are few; still, any undesirable behavior that stems from ill treatment can prove extremely difficult to eradicate.

Some horses do seem inherently more trusting than others, but I believe that trust is largely a learned behavior as opposed to an inherited trait. Friendly, trusting mares tend to have friendly, trusting foals; the offspring of skittish, flighty mares are likely to be the same way. Why? Because foals, like children, imitate their mothers and adopt their attitudes. A horse that is raised in a kind, loving atmosphere and that is handled from birth is likely to grow up liking people. With proper training, such a horse should develop a high level of trust in his rider. I am sure that my stallion, Giotto, has been treated kindly and gently since the day he was born. In turn, he responds kindly and gently to everyone he comes in contact with.

Assess Your Horse's Psyche

How great is your horse's trust in you? Is he a confident partner and performer? Your responses to the following questions will reveal a lot about his character. For each item, choose the response that most accurately describes your horse's behavior.

1. When you walk into your horse's stall, he usually:
   a) Pricks his ears and walks forward to greet you
   b) Retreats to the far corner of his stall
   c) Turns tail, pins his ears, and threatens to kick

2. If something frightens your horse and you reassure him with your voice and a pat, he usually responds by:
   a) Steadying himself
   b) Spooking into the next county
   c) Tensing

3. During training sessions, your horse's demeanor usually is:
   a) Relaxed and focused
   b) Worried
   c) Irritated

4. If you ask your horse to do something new, he tends to react by:
   a) Trying hard
   b) Tensing and "backing off"
   c) Fighting

5. When you praise your horse for something done well, he often responds by:
   a) "Puffing up" with self-satisfaction and trying even harder
   b) Momentarily relaxing, then tensing up again
   c) Acting irritated by your touch

If you answered mostly "a's," your horse probably has a high level of trust in you and confidence in himself and in his work. Strive to preserve his excellent attitude through careful training and handling.

If you answered mostly "b's," he hasn't quite learned to trust you completely and he's not too sure of himself, either. Patient and consistent work that never overfaces him should develop his trust and confidence over time.

If you answered mostly "c's," he is defensive and protective of himself; he may be suffering from past mistreatment. If your horse is exhibiting potentially dangerous behaviors, I urge you to seek the assistance of a professional trainer. You love your horse, but please don't get hurt trying to retrain him. A professional trainer may be able to help break bad behaviors and also can give you an educated opinion as to whether your horse is safe for you to handle and ride.

Set Your Goals

In your journal or notebook, write a sentence or two that describes a realistic goal regarding your horse's trust and confidence. Examples:

"When my horse feels anxious or unsure of himself, I want to soothe him so that he's noticeably calmed by my reassurances."

"To send my horse to a professional trainer for 30 days for evaluation, rehabilitation, and his or her opinion as to our suitability as partners."

Exercise

Spend lots of time with your horse, both mounted and unmounted. Learn his character and his natural tendencies. If he's skittish, be very calm and reassuring as you work around him. If he tends to be lazy, be peppy and enthusiastic in your demeanor.

Your horse can't learn to trust you if you just come to the barn, get on, ride, and leave. Trust takes time.

Progress Check

As you work toward achieving your goals regarding your horse's trust and confidence, do a progress check every seven to ten days. The following are good indicators of progress:

✔ Increased friendliness and willingness to walk up to you

✔ Decreased tension and spookiness, both on the ground and under saddle

✔ Decreased defensiveness, especially in the stall

✔ A more relaxed and positive demeanor while being handled, groomed, and tacked up

✔ A calming effect when you pat and reassure him

✔ (For hunters, jumpers, and event horses) fewer run-outs, refusals, or "chips"

✔ (For dressage, trail, and pleasure horses) increased relaxation; a feeling that he enjoys his work more than in the past.

ANSWERS TO QUESTIONS ON PAGE 112

   1. Tempo, rhythm, and suppleness
   2. Send the horse forward from the leg
   3. Causes the forward energy to "recycle" back to the hindquarters

How did you do? If you got all three right, you have a clear picture of how contact works. If you missed one or more questions, you need to brush up on your understanding of contact. Pay special attention to the exercises for this section, which begin on page 123.

ANSWERS TO QUESTIONS ON PAGE 113

   4.2–e; 4.3–d; 4.4–a; 4.5–c; 4.6–b.

Betsy's Tips

Consider the way that your horse feels about his environment. Horses can have likes and dislikes, anxieties and fears, just as we do. Imagine: If you were he, how would you feel about his situation? How would you handle it? Try to put yourself in his four shoes.

5.1
IMPULSION, *or schwung, is the lift and spring created by energetic, dynamic energy. Here is Giotto performing a flying change.*

CHAPTER FIVE

Building Block 4: *Impulsion*

Impulsion (im pul′shən), *n.*
1. the act of impelling, driving onward, or pushing. 2. the resulting state or effect; impulse; impetus. 3. the inciting influence of some feeling or motive; mental impulse.

"I t don't mean a thing if it ain't got that *schwung*."

Borrowing from the famous line from the song "It Don't Mean a Thing (If It Ain't Got that Swing)" will help you to remember the meaning—and the spirit—of the German word *schwung*, which literally translated means "swing." U.S. riders may be less familiar with the word *schwung* than they are with the more common American term, *impulsion*. The German National Equestrian Federation defines *schwung* as "the transmission of the energetic impulse created by the hind legs, into the forward movement of the entire horse." Just as a power plant synthesizes electricity from raw materials and chemical reactions, you produce *schwung* in your horse by synthesizing the impulses of your body and mind. Here's how it works.

RIDER

impulsion AND THE RIDER

The MIND Element: Energy

What You Need to Know

Before you can work on developing your horse's *schwung* or *impulsion*, you need to have a clear understanding of the concept of energy in the horse, and you need to know how to create it.

Some riders think, mistakenly, that "impulsion" means "forward"; and it is here that the concept of "swinging" can help clarify the intended meaning. As the late Dr. Reiner Klimke wrote in his book *Basic Training of the Young Horse*,

> With the help of contact we can improve the "schwung." A horse looks its best under a rider only when it is evident that the hindquarters push off with energy and spring, and that the power generated in trot or canter is conducted forward through the swinging rounded back of the horse—the horse is working "through." That is what we call "schwung."
>
> The aim in dressage is more "schwung" so that we have more expression to the movement. We like to cultivate the natural gaits, to give them more expression, balance, brilliance and cadence so that the horse can stay longer in the air, but without stiffness or flicking of the legs. Each leg must bend at the joints and step onto the ground where it points....
>
> "Schwung" enables the horse to move in the most expressive way that nature gave it. Some horses by nature have little expression, i.e., have flat gaits.... This means the horse must be able to use all four legs with maximum expression and to do this entails engaging the hind legs through muscling up the hindquarters so it is easy to engage them. Many people forget that the shoulders are also important and should not be stiff. They need to develop free movement. The expression comes from behind but if it cannot go through the back and through the shoulders because the shoulders are stiff then again there is no "schwung."[1]

As you may have surmised, the terms "impulsion" and "schwung" are greater than the sum of their parts. They encompass many qualities: pep and pizzazz,

---

[1] *USDF Manual*, p. 158. Reprinted with permission of J. A. Allen.

power and spring, snappy reactions, elasticity, and responsiveness. I like to simpli-fy this lengthy definition by thinking of impulsion as *dynamic energy*.

Impulsion is not the same thing as speed, and a horse performing a very col-lected movement may in fact have as much—if not more—impulsion than one doing a "knock your socks off" extended trot. Impulsion is power and energy, given freely when called for. Think about the difference between walking and marching: You're moving at the same speed when you do both, but one is more energetic and more animated. A horse with a lot of impulsion appears to bounce off the ground as he moves. His strides are powerful yet fluent and easy for the rider to sit, and his movement is joyous yet efficient.

With impulsion, your horse can easily extend or collect his strides. With impul-sion, he gives you more when you ask for it, without quickening his pace or chang-ing his rhythm or tempo; and he keeps giving you more when you ask him to take a shorter, loftier stride. In contrast, the movement of a horse without impulsion appears flat and jarring; and he tends to take short, quick, low-to-the-ground steps.

Impulsion exists only in the trot and the canter, which are the two gaits that have a moment of suspension. The walk lacks a moment of suspension and so, by definition, it cannot have impulsion.

As Dr. Klimke pointed out, impulsion should not be confused with flashy yet stiff movement. A common example is an incorrect extended trot characterized by dramatic "flicking" of the forelegs while the hind legs do relatively little. Some breeds of horses are known for showy movement with lots of knee and hock action, but such movement is not the same as impulsion, which requires power, spring, elasticity, and complete use of the back.

Assess Your Understanding

Take a look at the following photographs of horses in various gaits and movements (figs. 5.2 A – F). Some have *schwung*, while others do not.

Set Your Goals

In your journal or notebook, write a sentence or two that describes a realistic goal regarding your understanding of the concept of *schwung* or impulsion. Example:

"I will learn to tell the difference between *forward* and *impulsion*."

"I will work to feel and become aware of when my horse bends the joints in his hind legs and has greater lift off the ground."

5.2 A – F
Schwung
Here's Hilltop's Giotto in a pleasant warm-up trot but one that lacks schwung. He appears relatively earth-bound, his stride lacks energy from behind, and his poll is too low **(A)**.

This trot has plenty of schwung or impulsion. Giotto is round like a ball; he appears to bounce off the ground **(B)**.

Don't let Giotto's big movement fool you: This canter isn't really coming up off the ground with impulsion **(C)**.

Now Giotto's canter is much loftier and energetic **(D)**.

Continued:

E

5.2 A – F (cont.)

In this piaffe, Jane Clark's Rainier is showing his ability for schwung with the power, spring, and elasticity of his lowered haunches and active fore-hand **(E)**.

Tami Hoag's mare, Feliki, has "power-packed" haunches that let her express plenty of schwung in her passage **(F)**.

F

Exercises

EXERCISE 1: The Bouncing Exercise Ball

Acquainting yourself with the feeling a horse gives his rider as he bounces off the ground with impulsion is easy and fun: Simply sit on an exercise ball and bounce gently. The ball "gives" under your seat as you bounce down and then lifts you back up. The movement is fluent and rhythmical. A horse that's moving with schwung will give you a very similar feeling (figs. 5.3 A – D and figs. 5.4 A – D).

5.3 A – D
*Here's the effect of the "bouncing ball" in motion. Giotto shows a swinging balanced trot (**A**), a trot extension (**B**), in canter (**C**) his haunches balance underneath himself repeating the "bouncing-ball" effect, and in (**D**) he begins to lower his haunches and lift his forehand.*

5.4 A – D
Impulsion
*This series of photos shows Giotto really using his haunches and lifting his shoulders, demonstrating his impulsion. Photo **(C)** shows an exaggerated lift of the forehand. Photo **(D)** shows how that energy lifts up and away from the ground.*

EXERCISE 2: Video and Research Study

Get a videotape of an Olympic Games, World Cup, or World Championship dressage competition. Watch the way that the horses spring off the ground. Train your eye to see how the joints of the horses' hind legs bend, how they use their backs, and how their movement flows gracefully through their shoulders. The movement should appear harmonious, powerful, and exciting. Then watch horses go at home or at shows. Compare their movement to what you saw on the international-competition videotapes.

Another great resource is famed Finnish rider, trainer, and clinician Kyra Kyrklund's discussion of *schwung* in her six-videotape set, *Training with Kyra Kyrklund*.

Finally, it's helpful to learn about equine biomechanics—how horses move, and what they do with their bodies when we ask them to collect, extend, bend, move laterally, and so on. Dr. Hilary Clayton, holder of the Mary Anne McPhail Dressage Chair in Equine Sports Medicine at Michigan State University, is the world's most famous equine-biomechanics expert. She regularly contributes articles on her research to dressage magazines and also posts research findings and information on the McPhail Chair's website: http://cvm.msu.edu/dressage.

Progress Check

Go back and review the series of photographs on page 146 to 148. After 30 days of studying horses' movement in person or on videotape, are you better able to tell the difference between a horse with impulsion, power, and spring and a "flat" mover whose energy is not coming through from behind? If you answered yes, you're well on your way to understanding the concept of *schwung* more fully.

The BODY Element: Core Strength with Power

What You Need to Have

Because you've read this far, you already know that your seat is the most important part of your body in riding, and the most important aid. You've probably read and heard countless other experts discuss the importance of a "strong seat" or a "secure seat." Well, what exactly *is* the seat, in anatomical terms?

Your seat is much more than the part of you that makes contact with the saddle. I think of the rider's seat as all of the muscles in the abdomen, lower back,

Betsy's Tips

Human athletes as well as horses can have schwung. Picture basketball star Michael Jordan in action. Jordan's gymnastic ease and grace, combined with his power and energy, enable him to perform leaps that seem to defy gravity. That combination of suppleness, flowing movement, channeled energy, and power is his schwung; and it makes him able to jump higher and more swiftly than most other players.

The same concept applies to the legendary ballet dancer Mikhail Baryshnikov, who can go from standing still to a seemingly impossible leap in a split second and with little apparent effort. He has the ability to store energy and then explode skyward while remaining relaxed and completely in control of his muscular effort.

gluteal (buttock) muscles, hips, and upper legs. What riders call the "seat" other athletes call the "trunk," the "core," or the "powerhouse." These large muscles act as the trunk of a tree: They stabilize and support your "branches," or extremities. Your abdominal muscles, in particular, hold your upper body erect, help you to maintain your balance, control your center of gravity, and support and work in harmony with the muscles of your lower back. In the saddle, your abdominals work in concert with the other trunk muscles to absorb the shock of your horse's movement, to keep your seat secure and quiet, to give the aids for half-halts and halts, and to enable you to "go with" the motion, to name a few of their most important functions. Because of the seat's incredible range of influence over the horse's pace and way of going, it plays a critical role in the development and maintenance of impulsion. The seat is "ground zero" for the creation of impulsion.

Many riders, like many of the general population, have weak abdominal and "trunk" muscles. It is an unfortunate but true fact that many complaints of common lower-back pain could be alleviated or entirely eliminated through a program of core-strength development. Most riders who have difficulty sitting the trot, complain that riding hurts their backs, or who lack a secure, elegant seat could benefit from the development of a stronger trunk or core.

Assess Your Skill Level

Ask yourself the following questions. If you answer no to one or more, you may benefit from a fitness program designed to strengthen your core.

1. Do you find it difficult to sit the trot?
2. Do you suffer from lower-back pain, especially during or after riding?
3. Do you tend to "collapse" at the waist in the saddle?
4. Do you lose your balance and fall forward if your horse pulls on the reins?
5. Can you perform 20 abdominal crunches while maintaining correct form?

Set Your Goals

In your journal or notebook, write a sentence or two that describes a realistic (remember, "realistic" means "achievable within 30 days") goal regarding the development of your core strength with power. Examples:

"To experience a noticeable difference in my ability to sit the trot."

"To learn what I can do if I experience lower-back pain while I'm riding."

"To be able to use the muscles of my 'trunk' to produce noticeably more impulsion in my horse."

Exercises

As a rider, you need to be able to separate the movement of your spine from that of your hips. The hip joint is separate from the spine, and moving the hips without moving the back—a concept known as *hip dissociation*—is biomechanically correct and the most efficient way to move. Hip dissociation also allows the rider's seat to push and to create power through the use of the gluteal muscles.

Unfortunately, many riders, through faulty positioning of the hips and spine, lack of training and flexibility, or as the result of a fall or other trauma, are not able to separate the movement of the hips from that of the spine. This is known as *hip association*. In hip association, movement of the hips causes the lower back to move. When the lower back moves, energy is transmitted up the spine and into the shoulders, almost like a shock wave. The constant irritation to the lower back is a common cause of recurrent and chronic lower-back pain.

The *Pilates* exercises that follow promote hip dissociation and encourage a wider range of movement of the leg within the hip socket. They'll also help to develop your seat and to reinforce quick, powerful moves.

EXERCISE 1: Femur Circles

Start by lying on your back with both knees bent in the air over your hips and your hands on top of your knees. Attain a neutral pelvis position. Inhale and use your hands to guide your knees toward your chest. Without losing the neutral pelvis, circle your knees away from each other and then back together. Repeat the exercise in the opposite direction. As you circle your knees, make sure that you keep your tailbone pointing down toward the floor, maintaining a neutral pelvis (figs. 5.5 A – C).

EXERCISE 2: Leg Circles

Lie on your back with your right leg straight and pointed at the ceiling and your left foot on the floor with your knee bent. Attain a neutral pelvis with your core engaged. Inhale as you take your right leg to the right side of your body and then

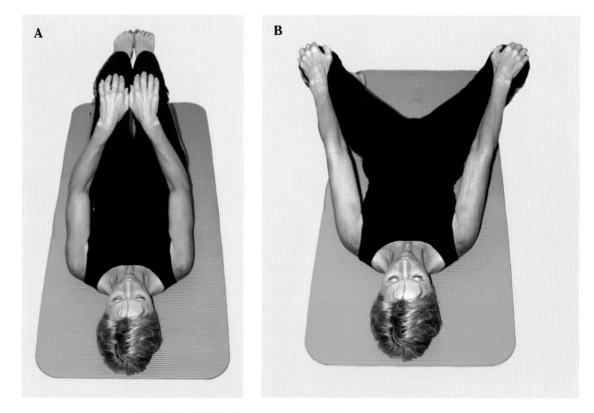

5.5 A – C
Femur Circles
I start on my back with both knees bent over my hips, hands on my knees, and engaging my core **(A)**.

Maintaining a neutral pelvis, I circle my knees downward and away from each other, while using my core to stabilize my hips **(B)**.

I continue the exercise by circling my knees back up and away from each other coming back to my original position **(C)**. *My focus throughout the exercise is on stabilizing my core.*

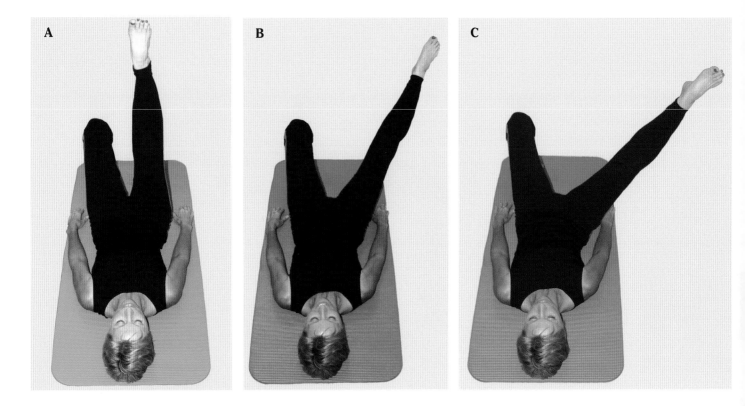

circle it down and around to the side; exhale as you bring it back up to the starting position. Make sure that your left hip does not lift off the floor; you'll need to use your core muscles—especially your left oblique abdominals—to hold your left knee aligned with your left hip and left shoulder, while your right leg circles. Make only as large a circle as you can manage while keeping your hips down and still. Make sure that your left knee stays aligned with your left hip and does not sway outward as your right leg circles. Circle the leg in the opposite direction and then switch legs. Circle each leg five times in each direction (figs. 5.6 A – C).

EXERCISE 3: Side Leg Lifts

Lie on your side with both legs straight and your hips "stacked" on top of each other. Attain a neutral pelvis with your core engaged. Position your supporting shoulder over your elbow, and slide your shoulder blade back and down, away from your ear. Try not to "load" (put all your weight on) the shoulder. Raise your lower ribs so that they do not sag; think axial elongation. Inhale and raise your top leg, keeping your lower ribs up. Exhale and lower the top leg to the starting posi-

5.6 A – C
Leg Circles
Starting position for leg-circle exercise **(A)**.

Start by making the leg circles only as large as you can manage while keeping the opposite hip down on the floor **(B)**.

As you gain flexibility and mobility in your hip joint, you'll be able to make larger circles while keeping your hips still, as I'm demonstrating here **(C)**.

5.7 A & B
Side Leg Lifts
Starting position for side leg lifts **(A)**.

Keep your hips "stacked" one over the other, and use your gluteal muscles to power the lift and to control the lowering of your free leg **(B)**.

tion. It's less important that you lift your leg very high than it is that you're able to keep your lower ribs up during the movement. Do five repetitions and then switch sides (figs. 5.7 A & B).

For Advanced Pilates Students: Work on the Reformer

Use the reformer only if you are familiar with the apparatus or if you are under the supervision of a certified *Pilates* instructor. The exercises below are not designed for beginners or for people with no reformer experience. If you do not have previous reformer experience, work with a certified *Pilates* instructor until you feel comfortable working on the equipment on your own.

5.8
Hamstring Arcs
Starting position for the hamstring-arc exercise. I'm lying on the Pilates reformer, arms at my sides, with my feet in the straps and my legs perpendicular to the ground.

EXERCISE 4: Hamstring Arcs

Lie on the reformer with your head in the headrest and both feet in the straps (fig. 5.8). Make sure that your shoulders are not jammed up against the shoulder rest. Slide your shoulder blades down, away from your ears, with your hands reaching for your feet. Use a resistance that is not so heavy that you have to "muscle" through the movement, but not so light that it is too easy. Make sure that your pelvis is in neutral position. Inhale and lift your legs into the air; exhale and lower your legs, initiating the movement from your core and completing it with your hamstrings. Use your core muscles, not your glutes, to accomplish the movement. Lower your legs until they are parallel with the floor, keeping your lower back from arching (5.9). Inhale and raise your legs up toward the ceiling, thinking of lifting through the longest curve possible. Do five repetitions of each of the following: toes in neutral, toes out/heels together, and toes in/heels out. Resist the temptation to let your pelvis tip into a posterior pelvis position when your legs lift into the air.

5.9
Engaging my abdominal muscles, I use my core muscles (not my glutes) to lower my legs as far as I can while keeping my lower back from arching off the reformer.

EXERCISE 5: Leg Circles

This is the same exercise as Number 2 above, only on the reformer. The principles of the exercise remain the same. On the reformer, exhale and lower your legs until they are parallel with the reformer; then circle them around until they are reaching toward the ceiling. Do five clockwise circles and five counterclockwise circles with each leg.

For a nice hamstring stretch, raise your legs as high as you can while keeping your tailbone down and your pelvis in neutral position.

EXERCISE 6: The Inverted V

Place your feet flat on the reformer with your heels up against the shoulder rests. Place your hands on the footbar with your wrists in neutral positionænot bent backward (fig. 5.10). (*Caution: Pilates* is not very forgiving on the wrists, so be careful to not weight-bear more than necessary. You can shift your body weight back into your hips, and off your wrists.) Slide your shoulder blades down and back, away from your ears. Bring your chest as close to your legs as possible while raising your tailbone toward the ceiling; for those of you who have studied yoga, this position is similar to the Downward Dog. Exhale and push the carriage back, using your hamstrings and core—not your arms—until you feel your heels raising off the carriage. Press your heels down, lift your tailbone toward the ceiling, and bring your chest closer to your legs. As you inhale, draw the carriage back to the starting position, using your core to get your feet back under your chest (fig. 5.11). You will feel a stretch in your hamstrings and possibly in your calves. Do five repetitions.

For a greater hamstring stretch, use more springs on the reformer. For a greater emphasis on the core, use fewer springs.

EXERCISE 7: The Jackrabbit

This exercise is the same as the Inverted V, except that your toes are on the carriage and your heels are up on the shoulder pads (fig. 5.12). As you exhale, push the carriage back with your hamstrings and core until you are in a full plank (extended) position. Keeping your back flat, inhale, bringing your knees under your hips without rolling your hips under (fig. 5.13). Exhale, funnel the ribs and engage the core to straighten your legs back into a full plank position. Do five repetitions. Make sure that your core and your legs—not your arms—do most of the work.

For more leg work, use more springs on the reformer. For more core work, use fewer springs.

5.10
The Inverted V
Starting position for the Inverted V exercise. I'm standing on the reformer while holding on to the footplate. My legs, back, and arms are straight; and my back, neck, head, and arms are aligned.

5.11
Keeping my upper body aligned, I use my core muscles and legs to slide the carriage back and then to bring the carriage back to starting position as I draw in my core.

5.12

The Jackrabbit

The starting position for the Jackrabbit is similar to the ending position for the Inverted V, except that here I've extended my body all the way into a full plank position.

5.13

In Step 2 of the Jackrabbit, I bend my knees and bring the carriage under my hips until my thighs are perpendicular to the floor.

What happens? If he's engaging his hindquarters correctly, you'll feel a surge of power and a lifting beneath your seat as he bends his hind legs and pushes off more energetically—all without quickening his pace or becoming heavy in your hands. If his response is to go faster, you may feel as if you're suddenly steering a freight train, and you'll probably feel more weight in your hands as he falls on his forehand and leans on the bit for balance. If he's lazy, you might not get much of a response at all!

Set Your Goals

In your journal or notebook, write a sentence that describes a realistic goal regarding your horse's understanding of power and activity. Examples:

"I will work to bring my horse into balance so that he's able to take a more powerful stride rather than speeding up."

"I will improve my horse's promptness in responding to my driving aids."

Exercises

EXERCISE 2: Tempo Changes for Energy

The following exercise combines bending with a change in tempo. Establish a regular and rhythmic sitting trot at A (working or collected, depending on your horse's level of training) on a 20-meter circle. Using your seat, give a half-halt and ask him to go forward in medium trot for half the diameter of the circle. Now, control your seat again by using your lower back and abdominals. Feel as though you close your leg from your hip, through your upper leg, to your knee; and allow that flow of energy to hold his stride upward, bringing him into a slower and more collected trot for a few strides. As you slow his motion, strive for the feeling that his hind end quickens while his front end slows and lifts. Take your time to develop some good, steady, balanced, and more collected strides; this is accomplished by pushing him toward the reins, not by pulling back. Once he's balanced in collected trot, push him forward into an extended trot. Think of asking for power in shorter spurts—as quick bursts of energy. Your horse should burst forward off your leg. Using the same principles, you can also try this exercise in the canter.

In the second part of the exercise, go down the long side of the arena in a forward trot (medium or extended, depending on your horse's degree of advancement). Let's say you're tracking left. Ride extended trot from F to R. Carefully ride

5.14
Tempo Changes for Energy

This exercise works on getting your horse to give you quick and immediate responses to your aids, and builds power with the bursts of energy. See the text for details of the movements.

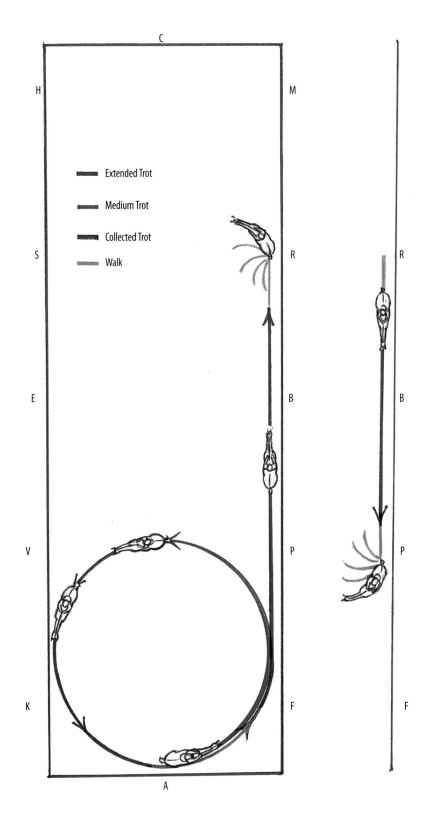

a transition to walk a few steps before R and do a quiet, deliberate, step-by-step turn on the haunches. The moment that he is straight on the long side, ask for a quick response back into the extended trot by dropping your seat down into the saddle in the first trot step, keeping a firm seat. In the second trot step, give a "bounce" with your lower legs while you relax your fingers for a step or two, then close your fingers and push forward into medium trot. You want his reactions to be quick and immediate. Your seat will have to be very effective, and you will learn how to drive securely and energetically as well as to "hold and allow" with your seat as you repeat the walk-turn on the haunches-trot sequence again at P (fig. 5.14). This helps to lower your horse's haunches and teach him the correct and alert response to your seat and leg. After you're comfortable with this exercise in the trot, go ahead and try it in the canter; the walking elements of the exercise remain the same.

EXERCISE 2: Shoulder-In

This classic gymnastic exercise is excellent for teaching the correct use of the hind legs, and improves the horse's suppleness, balance, and strength. The shoulder-in is one of the best all-around gymnastic exercises. Being able to do a good shoulder-in is the conduit to tie your gymnastic work into actual movements.

In the shoulder-in, the horse bends around the rider's inside leg just enough to bring his forehand slightly to the inside of the track (the line of travel). To do this, he must lighten his forehand and increase the flexibility and activity of his hind legs. If he does the exercise correctly, he will "fill" the outside rein nicely, and his body will be positioned between the rider's inside leg and outside rein, with the inside rein gently encouraging inside flexion and the outside leg keeping his haunches from swinging to the outside. The control established by bringing the inside hind leg directly under the horse's haunches will provide the power to produce impulsion.

Prepare for the shoulder-in by riding on a 20-meter trot circle at one end of the arena. Ride a little more deeply into the second corner. As you come out of the corner, ride one stride off the track (as if you were going back onto the circle); but instead of following the circle, go straight down the long side of the arena, striving to maintain that slight bend and inside flexion. Feel the bend and flexion truly connect into your outside rein. Think of bringing your horse's forehand up in front of you and around your inside leg as you hold his haunches on the track. Imagine that

5.15
Shoulder-In

The idea behind this exercise is to "fill" the outside rein by pushing the horse's body into an imagined line of string running from the horse's outside hip diagonally across the arena, and let the string "pull" the horse's shoulder toward M while you move down the long side.

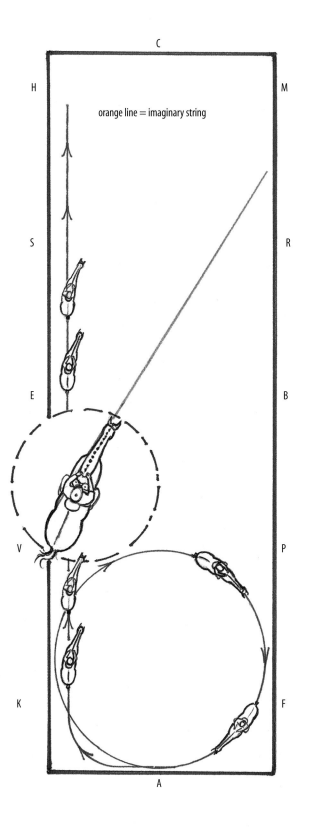

a string is attached to his outside hip, shoulder, and outside rein and stretches across the arena in a diagonal line. Using your seat and legs, keep pushing the line of his body into that imaginary string so that it fills up the inside rein (fig. 5.15).

As with all gymnastic work, it's important to do the shoulder-in exercise in equal amounts in both directions. When done correctly, it will really connect your horse's haunches to his forehand. This is a difficult exercise to do correctly, especially if your horse has a weak back or hindquarters, so be happy with just a few strides of shoulder-in before you straighten him by softening your inside flexion and using both legs into your outside rein.

Common mistakes in the shoulder-in (fig 5.16 b to e):

▶ Using inside leg but not enough outside rein or leg, so the haunches or shoulders "fall" to the outside (5.16b).

▶ Pulling the horse's head and neck to the inside with the inside rein but not truly bending him by pushing his rib cage into your outside rein with your inside leg (5.16c).

▶ Bringing the horse's forehand too far to the inside, which forces him into a leg-yield instead of a true shoulder-in (5.16d). (The difference? In shoulder-in, the outside foreleg and inside hind leg remain on the same "track" or line of movement.)

▶ Placing or leaning your weight to the outside, which forces your horse to step to the outside in an attempt to balance underneath your weight on the outside, instead of keeping your seat balanced in the saddle (5.16e).

Progress Check

As you work toward your initial 30-day goal, evaluate your progress every week to ten days with the following assessment items. (Ask your instructor or a knowledgeable friend for his or her opinion if you're not sure.)

✔ Can your horse maintain his inside bend and flexion down the long side in shoulder-in without "falling" to the inside or the outside?

✔ Can he do shoulder-in without slowing his normal trot rhythm and tempo?

✔ Can you soften your inside rein for a few strides without your horse losing his inside bend? If he immediately straightens his head and neck when you give the inside rein, you're pulling him to the inside; he's not truly bent around your inside leg and accepting the outside-rein contact.

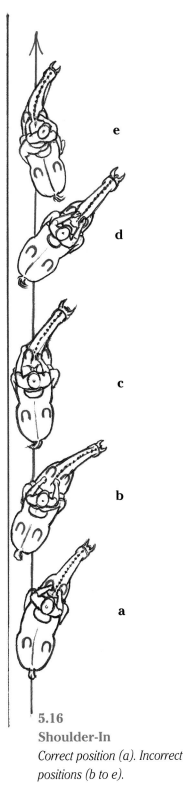

5.16
Shoulder-In
Correct position (a). Incorrect positions (b to e).

Betsy's Tips

As you develop your horse's power and activity correctly with the shoulder-in exercise, you will feel as if your lower back has become more elastic. Your horse's gaits will become easier to sit, and yet you'll get a feeling of power and "roundness" as he moves underneath you in a more organized, connected way. He may feel as if he grows bigger and taller in front of the saddle (because his forehand and withers lift), while the area behind the saddle (his haunches) seems to become more compact.

✔ Can he do shoulder-in equally well in both directions? (If not, don't panic. Horses are like people—they're left-sided or right-sided the way we are left-handed or right-handed—and one side most likely will be stronger than the other. Your goal is to make his sides even.)

The BODY Element: Energy

What Your Horse Needs to Have

As your horse learns to bend the joints of his hind legs and to step well underneath himself in response to your driving aids, his body begins to develop the physical energy that will be transformed into impulsion. Remember the discussions of the "muscle ring" in the last chapter? It's this cyclical impulse that enables him to channel his energy into thrust and suspension—the beginnings of what is known as "carrying power," which later on becomes collection.

At this stage of his training, it is even more important that your horse develop a harmonious blend of strength and suppleness: strength, to give his hindquarters the power to carry more weight and take more active strides and his abdominal and back muscles to lift and swing; and suppleness, to allow the energy to come over his topline and his paces to remain regular and even. Insufficient strength can lead to irregularity of the paces; a common example is the horse asked to extend the trot and falling into an incorrect rhythm in which one diagonal pair of legs may take a longer or shorter stride than the other. Insufficient suppleness can lead to tension in the topline, neck, or jaw and the resulting jarring gait and "flicked" forelegs; it is also a prime contributor to back soreness in both horse and rider.

Assess Your Horse's Skill Level

Use the following checklist to evaluate your horse's ability to create and sustain physical energy.

1. Does your horse move forward instantly off your leg aids?
2. Can he manage transitions between a working or collected gait into a more forward lengthening or extension of his strides without his gait becoming irregular?

3. Does he remain soft and supple when you apply your driving aids to ask for more impulsion?

4. Does he remain round and springy when you ask for more impulsion?

If you answered no to one or more of the above, you need to rev up his energy level.

Set Your Goals

In your journal or notebook, write a sentence or two that describes a realistic goal regarding the development of your horse's physical energy. Examples:

"When I put my leg against my horse, I expect him to move instantly forward."

"In 30 days, my horse will be able to sustain a lengthening halfway across the diagonal without flattening and falling onto his forehand."

"I will develop my horse's strength and suppleness so that he is able to remain soft within the impulsion."

Exercises

The following three exercises build on the shoulder-in. These simple variations can be adjusted to suit your horse's level of development and are great for building your horse's strength, suppleness, and energy.

EXERCISE 1: Shoulder-In to Shallow Serpentine in Trot

In the trot, do shoulder-in from K to V. At V, send your horse on the diagonal to X and then back to H in a shallow serpentine. Your outside (left) rein will become your inside rein during the X-to-H loop of the serpentine, a good test of your horse's acceptance of both reins. Later, when his balance and strength have improved sufficiently, add a ten-meter circle at H (fig. 5.17).

Be sure to do this exercise in both directions so that you develop your horse's energy, balance, strength, and suppleness evenly on both sides of his body.

EXERCISE 2: Shoulder-In to Diagonal in Trot.

Ride shoulder-in in trot from K to V. From V, go across a diagonal line (from V to M). Ask your horse to lengthen or extend his strides from V to M. He'll need to use his inside hind leg actively in the shoulder-in, and move well into the outside (left)

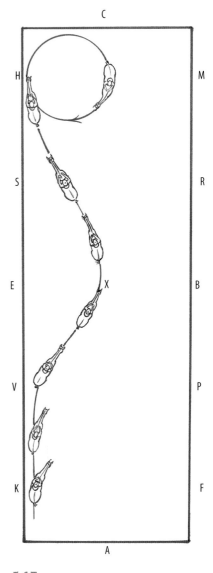

5.17
Shoulder-In to a Shallow Serpentine
In trot, use this exercise to improve your horse's and your own dexterity by changing the supporting outside rein. The result should be a softer, more elastic feel through your hands into the reins.

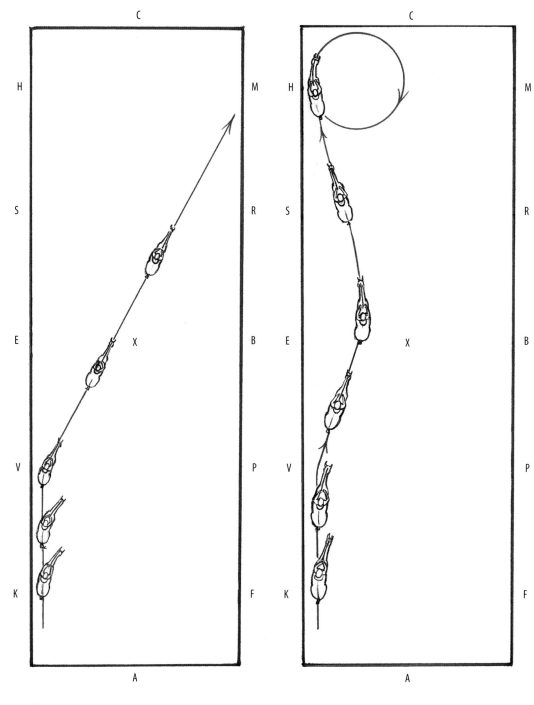

5.18
Shoulder-In to a Diagonal in Trot
After you've established a connected, elastic feeling in the reins, you can begin to develop more power from the haunches.

5.19
Shoulder-Fore in Canter
This exercise develops balance and power.

rein, in order to straighten promptly and generate the thrust he'll need to power across the diagonal while maintaining his balance and rhythm. You will need to have a well-balanced position and to support him with your outside leg as you begin the lengthening. Slow down and collect before the corner. Repeat in the opposite direction (fig. 5.18).

EXERCISE 3: Shoulder-Fore in Canter

It is difficult for horses to execute a correct shoulder-in in the canter, so a common gymnastic exercise is the "shoulder-fore," which is like the shoulder-in but with less bend plus inside positioning of the forehand. In this exercise, do shoulder-fore from K to V. At V, leave the rail and canter straight until you reach the quarter line (the distance halfway between the rail and the centerline) opposite X. Remain on the same canter lead (you'll now be in counter-canter) and gently curve back, reaching the rail at H. Keep a feel of your outside (left) rein to support your horse through the exercise, and keep your legs and upper body positioned for right-lead canter. When he is able to manage the shoulder-fore and gentle counter-canter exercise with ease, add a ten-meter circle at H. The idea here is that, with each segment of these exercises, you create a new surge of energy. Repeat in the opposite direction (fig. 5.19).

Progress Check

The above exercises will serve as their own progress checks. You'll know you're on the right track when your horse can do them while maintaining his:

- ✔ Rhythm and footfalls
- ✔ Tempo
- ✔ Suppleness
- ✔ Balance
- ✔ Connection
- ✔ Energy

The SPIRIT Element: Electric

What Your Horse Needs to Be

You may have heard trainers talk about wanting to make horses more "electric."

Betsy's Tips

Impulsion is a particular kind of energy. For your horse to have impulsion, he must have what I think of as power-packed joints. The energy is focused and is released in short spurts. Think of the energy of a marathoner as compared to that of a gymnast. The marathoner's energy is steady and sustained over a long period of time, whereas the gymnast "explodes" with brief and extremely focused and controlled spurts of energy. The energy of impulsion is like that of the gymnast, and it must be developed in a similar method: using brief, repeated periods of effort.

What do they mean?

Ideally, an "electric" horse responds 100 percent to the lightest aid. There is no hesitation and no less than absolute effort. His energy is channeled according to the rider's direction. An electric horse gives his rider a feeling of sustained power; he does not explode like a lightning bolt and then fizzle out.

The Germans have a term, which has no exact English equivalent, for this concept: *durchlassigkeit*. In *Principles of Riding: The Official Handbook of the German National Equestrian Federation*, "durchlassigkeit" is described as "the horse's immediate willingness to obey the rider's aids without the slightest resistance…. The more the *durchlassigkeit* is improved, the quicker the horse will respond to more and more delicately applied aids. This will become most obvious in transitions and halts. The degree to which *durchlassigkeit* exists in a horse is the measure of the correctness with which the training programme has been applied."[2]

"Hot" horses tend to be more electric than phlegmatic ones, but "electric" does not imply nervousness or tension. A tense horse may spook or bolt, but these actions are not electric because they are not channeled and controlled energy, and they are not done in response to the rider's aids. Fortunately, hot horses can learn to control their energy; and lazy horses can be energized—although the former may always be more electric than the latter.

The development of electric and instantaneous responses is important at this stage of training because an enthusiastic, energetic mindset is the bridge between your own "mental impulsion" and your horse's physical energy. You get excited; he gets excited; his body responds with a powerful yet controlled surge of energy.

Assess Your Horse's Psyche

How high is your horse's wattage on the electricity scale? Finding out is easy. Ask yourself the following question.

If I put my leg on strongly, my horse will probably:

1. Take off

2. Increase his pace a little

3. Kick out or suck back

If you answered 2 or 3, you need to reassess the "wattage" of your horse's "electric current."

---

2 *USDF Manual*, p. 264. Reprinted with permission of Half Halt Press.

Set Your Goals

In your journal or notebook, write a sentence or two that describes a realistic goal regarding your horse's level of mental electricity. Examples:

"I will work toward channeling my horse's energy in a more focused and relaxed way."

"Having my horse understand that each effort is directed toward the "ideal.""

Exercise

Your state of mind has to be equal to your horse's. If you want snappy reactions from him, you need to be the same way.

Try this exercise. Really push your horse forward with active legs while you give the reins. By doing this, you're telling him, "All I want is forward." Let him go forward for a few strides before you bring him back. Establish the "forward" with no restrictions: Don't worry about what gait he's in, or about the fact that he's lost roundness or isn't on the bit. Repeat the sequence until he accepts the fact that he must respond to your aids in a responsive, electric manner.

Progress Check

As you work toward your initial 30-day goal, refer to the following checklist every week to ten days to assess your horse's progress.

- ✔ If he tends to be tense and hot, is he using his energy when *I* ask him to and not when the spirit moves him?
- ✔ If he tends to explode if he feels tense and pressured, has he learned to channel and sustain his energy instead of releasing it all in one "lightning bolt" explosion?
- ✔ If he tends to be lazy to the driving aids, has his response become more electric?
- ✔ Does he respond to my aids the first time I ask?
- ✔ Does he respond to a light aid?

Betsy's Tips

If your horse is really dull to the driving aids, an experienced ground person (ideally, your instructor) can help teach him the desired "electric" response with the judicious use of a longe whip. The whip never makes contact with the horse, and there is no waving and flourishing. Ask your helper to hold a longe whip and to stand in the middle of the circle, well away from your horse. Establish a 20-meter circle in trot or canter, and send your horse forward for a few strides every couple of revolutions. If the response is not enthusiastic and immediate, your helper moves the whip in the direction of the hindquarters, taking care not to crack the whip or to frighten your horse. You'll probably feel him surge forward or even break gait. Don't immediately pull him back down into the desired gait if he breaks; you'll be punishing him for a correct response. Eventually, he'll learn that he'd better move out smartly when you give the aids, and you'll get a feel for the desired energetic response. Tighten your abdominal muscles as he surges forward to keep your upper body going with his motion; if you're caught unawares, you may find yourself being left behind.

6.1 STRAIGHTNESS *is the alignment of the horse's structure from the ground up.*

CHAPTER SIX

Building Block 5: *Straightness*

Straightness (strāt′ ness), *n.*
1. without a bend, angle, or
curve; direct. 2. evenly formed
or set. 3. in the proper order
or condition. 4. continuous or
unbroken.

"Ride your horse forward and straighten him."
–Gustav Steinbrecht, *Gymnasium des Pferdes*.

In gymnastic-training terms, *straightness* doesn't necessarily mean traveling in a straight line (although a correctly trained horse can indeed do that); rather, "straightness" means "alignment of the horse's structure." When a horse is traveling straight—whether on a straight line or a curved line—the line of travel bisects his spine and the muscles of his back and neck, and his muscles are stretched in a complementary way over the structure of his body.

The German National Equestrian Federation explains the concept of straightness in detail in its official handbook, *Principles of Riding*:

> *The horse's propulsive force, developed by the quarters, can only be fully utilized in forward direction if the horse moves "straight." A horse is "straight" if the hind feet follow exactly the same line as the front feet [figs. 6.2 A & B]. Only then can the rider transfer more weight evenly onto both hind legs increasing their carrying power.*
>
> *Most horses' bodies are naturally crooked. This is even more pronounced because a horse is narrower in his shoulders than in his hips [fig. 6.3]. Most horses move with their right hind leg outside and alongside the track of the right front leg. The propulsive force of this right hind leg moves diagonally across to the horse's left shoulder, transferring additional weight onto the left*

---

1 *USDF Manual*, p. 262. Reprinted with permission of Half Halt Press.

6.2 A & B
Herant is traveling straight as he trots directly toward the camera **(A)**.

front leg and giving the rider a much stronger contact on the left rein. In this case the horse will also lean against the rider's right leg….

To **straighten a horse** *his forehand has to be brought squarely in front of his quarters. Logically, the forehand must be aligned with the quarters, and not vice versa, as it is in the quarters that all forward movement originates….*

The rider should begin to straighten a horse the moment that he starts listening to the aids. But specialized straightening training can only begin with the development of propulsive force and "schwung," because in straightening, the horse has to be ridden forward with determination.[1]

Just as you are right- or left-handed, your horse is "sided," with one side of his body stronger and more dominant than the other. You may have heard trainers or instructors say that every horse has a "stiff side" and a "hollow side." Most horses are "stiff" (convex) on their stronger, most dominant side (usually the left) and "hollow" (concave) on their weaker side (usually the right). Experts disagree on the cause of horses' "sidedness." Some believe that it is innate, like handedness. Others believe that it is caused by crookedness in the rider's body. Those who argue that stiffness is rider-caused point to the common phenomenon of a rider who complains, "All of the horses I ride are stiff on the same side." In my experience, I've found that most horses exhibit stiffness on one side or the other or seem to have an "easy side" and a "difficult side," which supports the argument that sidedness is an innate characteristic. However, riders' own sidedness can and does influence their horses. Fortunately, correct *gymnastic training* can help to develop and balance the strength, suppleness, and alignment of horses (and riders); and this equal development in turn produces straightness.

B

Here Giotto demonstrates straightness on a curved line. The arc of his body conforms to the arc of the curve **(B)**.

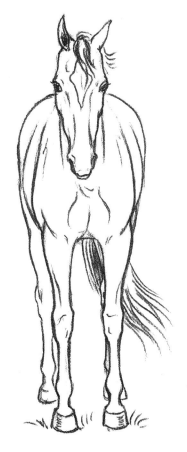

6.3

A horse is wider in his hips than in his shoulders. For the horse to be truly straight, you must always center his shoulders directly in front of his hips.

The MIND Element: Positioning

What You Need to Know

First, of course, you need to understand what straightness means as it's applied to your horse's body as well as to your own body, and how a horse can be straight (aligned) on both a straight line and a curve. Next, you need to have a clear understanding of how to use your aids to position your horse correctly to achieve straightness.

When a horse travels in a straight line or on a circle or turn, he is considered straight if his hind feet follow in the same "tracks" (lines of travel) as his forefeet. But, as I've explained, all horses display some degree of crookedness—and the fact that their hindquarters are wider than their shoulders further exaggerates the crookedness. Your job, then, is to teach your horse how to move straight—and to help him develop the equilateral balance, musculature, and flexibility to do so— through systematic gymnastic work. Much of that work entails *positioning* your horse in ways that will correct his crookedness and bring his shoulders into proper alignment with his haunches. Here are the basic principles of positioning.

First, to straighten your horse, position him so that his shoulders are slightly to the inside of ("leading") his haunches—not vice versa. This positioning requires him to bear more weight on his hind legs, particularly the inside hind, and therefore is a step toward developing the "carrying power" behind, which leads to the final building block of the training progression, *collection*. I'll discuss this in more detail in the following chapter.

The second aspect of positioning to achieve straightness is teaching your horse to close his hind legs laterally—in other words, to bring them closer to each other as he travels. This positioning helps to align the path of travel of the front and hind legs, which as you may recall is essential for him to be able to move straight. It also necessitates his bending the joints of his hind legs to a greater degree and, as a result, carrying more weight behind—both of which tie together the elements of impulsion and collection.

The third and final aspect of positioning is teaching your horse to close his hind legs longitudinally—in other words, to step further underneath his body. As he does so, he shifts his balance rearward and lifts or lightens his forehand; this will help to develop the "power-packed joints" that are so essential to impulsion and collection.

Although it may seem counterintuitive, the best way to straighten your horse is by using gymnastic lateral exercises (more about specific exercises on page 204). Just as stretching and strengthening exercises help your own body to become more powerful and supple, *gymnasticizing* exercises, performed correctly, help your horse to strengthen weak muscles and stretch tight ones, thus correcting imbalances that cause or contribute to crookedness. He will become more "pliable" on his stiff side and will be able to "fill out" his hollow side.

Assess Your Understanding

How well do you understand the concepts of positioning for straightness? Take the following quiz and find out.

1. In riding terms, "straight" is synonymous with:
   a) Parallel
   b) Aligned
   c) Traveling in a straight line

2. Part of the reason horses tend to travel crooked is that:
   a) They carry more weight on the forehand than over their hindquarters
   b) Their haunches are wider than their shoulders
   c) As a result of evolution, their feet and legs are too delicate for their size

3. Positioning for straightening work is:
   a) Haunches to the inside of the shoulders
   b) Shoulders to the inside of the haunches
   c) Haunches and shoulders in alignment

4. As part of achieving straightness, a horse has to learn to:
   a) Step sideways with his hind legs
   b) Bring his hind legs closer together
   c) Move his hind legs out behind him

Stumped? Turn to page 211 for the correct answers.

How did you do? If you answered all four correctly, you have a good basic understanding of the theories and principles of straightness. If you responded incorrectly to one or more items, go back and review pages 177-179. Then, in the next section, you'll have the opportunity to set goals for yourself to improve your understanding.

Set Your Goals

In your journal or notebook, write a sentence or two that describes a realistic goal regarding your understanding of positioning your horse in order to straighten him. Examples:

"To recognize the difference between straightness and crookedness on straight and curved lines."

"To recognize horses' stiff and hollow sides."

Exercises

EXERCISE 1: Observe and Apply

Watch horses go during lessons and schooling sessions. Watch haunches-out (renvers) being performed to see what happens; then do it to feel how the positioning of the movement makes your horse straight.

EXERCISE 2: Geometry Lessons

Learn the geometry of the dressage arena: where the various sizes of circles should begin and end, where the quarter lines are, and so on. Know what line you're riding on, and strive to ride every figure accurately.

EXERCISE 3: Position Check

No matter what movement you're riding, always position your horse's shoulders so that they're inside of ("leading") his haunches. Realize that "inside" and "outside" are relative terms; the shoulders should lead the haunches—relative to the line of travel—even in such movements as haunches-in.

EXERCISE 4: Ride by Feel

At this point in your training as a rider, you have to learn to ride more by feel and less by what you see in front of you. To do this, work to develop a keen sense of the activity and positioning of your horse's haunches. As you ride, think of holding the energy underneath you, balancing and positioning his shoulders, and positioning him in front of you.

Progress Check

At any place in the ring, in any gait, and during any movement, can you position your horse's shoulders inside of his haunches?

To straighten your horse, you must be very straight in your own body. You also need to be keenly aware of pushing him from back to front as well as from your inside leg to your outside rein while holding his shoulder in place with your outside upper leg and establishing flexion with your inside rein.

The BODY Element: Alignment

What You Need to Have

Alignment is the combination of coordination, core strength, balance, and timing as they work together throughout your entire body. When your body is aligned properly, it remains in balance with your horse's every move. The line of your hips remains parallel to the line of your horse's hips, your shoulders remain parallel to his shoulders, and your spine remains in the same line as his spine.

Alignment is a dynamic thing because motion is involved. You are a living, moving rider on a living, moving horse. An ideal does exist, but that ideal is ever-changing and requires a constant flow of energy, strength, and flexibility. To illustrate this concept, think of a gymnast on a balance beam. She's constantly adjusting her balance and alignment as she tries to maintain the effortless "centering" that allows her to move freely. If her body becomes misaligned with the balance beam, she falls off.

There are three types of alignment: your own body alignment, which has only to do with you and the control you have over your body; your horse's alignment, which results from your support and aid (more on this concept on page 201); and the alignment of horse and rider, acting as one harmonious entity. There are moments, if only for a stride, during which you feel that you're sitting inside your horse, rather than on top of him. You feel as if you are a part of him, and you move with him as one. In such moments, you are experiencing complete and harmonious alignment, whether you're feeling a few "right" steps in the sitting trot, a fluid pirouette, or going over a jump.

Balance goes hand in hand with alignment. You can achieve balance only if

Betsy's Tips

If you're standing directly in front of a horse that's working on a straight line, you should see only his two front legs because, if he's straight, his hind legs will be directly behind his forelegs. In addition, his head and the base of his neck should be centered between his shoulders, and his shoulders should be level. The same principles hold true if you view him from a position directly behind him: You should see only his hind legs, and his hips should be level with the dock of his tail centered between them. If you see more than two legs, or if his hips or shoulders are uneven, chances are he's crooked.

Of course, the above guidelines apply only if the horse is supposed to be traveling in a straight line. If he is doing a lateral movement such as shoulder-fore or shoulder-in, three legs will be visible because of the inside displacement of his shoulders, which places his inside hind leg on the same line of travel or "track" as his outside foreleg. (That's why normal travel is sometimes referred to as "movement on two tracks," and suppling exercises such as shoulder-in and haunches-in are called "three-track movements.")

your body is aligned properly. Balance is determined by your "center," a spot located two inches below your navel and midway between your navel and your spine. Your center functions like the trunk of a tree to support your body and to maintain your balance as you move. As you ride, work from your center, just as you want your horse to work from his center—his back. If you carry your weight in your chest and shoulders, your horse will probably do the same. If your weight shifts from side to side, he will be forced to keep rebalancing himself from side to side to compensate for your changing center of gravity. In short, he won't be straight.

This is how your alignment and balance relates to the building block of straightness. With the possible exception of a young horse, whose balance and strength isn't fully developed, your horse's crookedness usually mirrors your own misalignments and imbalances. If his haunches aren't coming sufficiently underneath him to carry his weight, the problem usually is that you are not carrying your own "haunches" underneath yourself; that is, you are probably relying too much on your arms and shoulders to position his head, rather than relying on your seat and legs to ride him from back to front. We riders have to carry our bodies in the same form that we want our horses to carry their bodies. The structural integrity from the horse's back regulates his limbs, but structural integrity has to be in place in the rider to allow that.

Body alignment is a complex concept that comprises several elements, including:

- *Core stability (abdominal and lower-back strength).*
- *Equal distribution of weight in the saddle*: Your upper body should be balanced over your hips and seat. You should have equal weight on both seat bones and in both reins, legs, and heels (fig. 6.4).
- *Correct equitation and postural alignment*: As viewed from the side, your shoulder, hip, and heel should be on the same vertical line. As viewed from the rear, you must sit in the middle of the saddle (not off to one side), with your upper body vertical (figs. 6.5 A – G).
- *Equal strength on both sides of the body*: Your left and right arms, hands, and legs should be equally strong.
- *Ambidexterity*: You need to be able to keep the same amount of grip on both reins to be able to "feel" your horse's mouth.

6.4
Alignment

My weight is distributed equally in the saddle. I'm sitting evenly on both seat bones and have equal weight in both reins, legs, and heels.

Rider's Tip: *Remember this alignment is possible by engaging your core and allowing hip stabilization.*

6.5 A – G
*Side view of correct posture in the
saddle: My shoulder, hip, and heel are
on the same vertical line* **(A)**.

*Without the use of core strength my
back has become arched, which is
throwing my upper body forward and
causing my position to become unsta-
ble. I can easily be pulled forward in
the saddle* **(B)**.

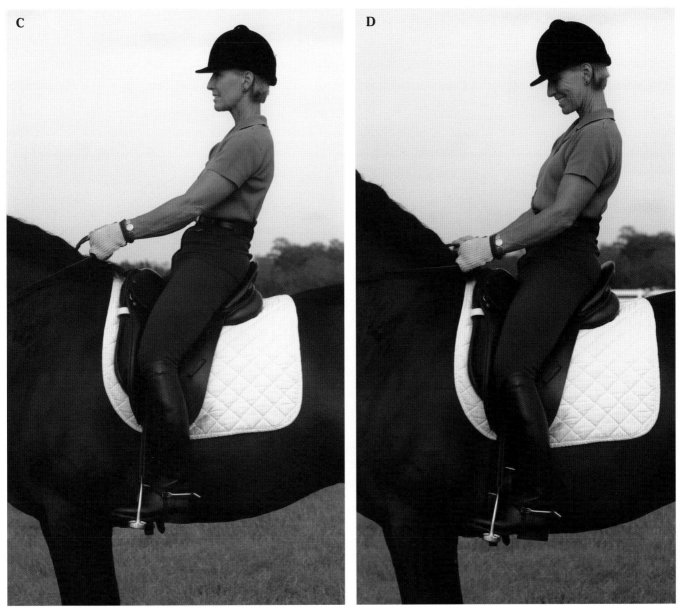

The classic "chair seat": I'm slumped
back in the saddle, my core muscles
slack and my waist collapsed, which
causes my legs to swing forward **(C)**.

Looking down, a common fault,
breaks your body alignment and
throws you out of balance—which will
make it difficult for your horse to balance and be aligned in his body **(D)**.

Continued:

E

F

6.5 A – G (cont.)
Because I have collapsed my right hip,
I've lost my core alignment, causing
my left shoulder to drop and my head
to tilt left in compensation **(E)**.

This exaggerated position will not help
me do a half-pass correctly **(F)**.

G

A very important part of position is the connection from seat to hand. Although my upper body has come a bit forward, there is a good connection from my elbow to Giotto's mouth in this downward beat of the canter stride **(G)**.

Several factors can cause you to become misaligned. Unequal strength—usually resulting from overuse of the dominant hand and side and underuse of the other—is perhaps the most common and can lead to a multitude of challenges, but fortunately, it's relatively simple to correct. Overall lack of strength is another common contributing factor and can lead to poor posture and incorrect riding position. Spinal misalignment can cause your hips to become unlevel, and your body can become misaligned as a result.

Assess Your Skill Level

How good are your body alignment, posture, and ambidexterity? Take the following quiz to find out.

Make a list, and for each item, note a "T" if the statement is usually true for you, and an "F" if the statement is usually false for you.

1. My instructor constantly tells me to let go of one rein.
2. If I look at myself in a mirror while I'm riding or watch a videotape of myself, I notice that I tend to sit off to one side of the saddle.
3. I have difficulty keeping my reins even.
4. I can't seem to use one leg as strongly and effectively as the other.
5. I tend to lose one or both of my stirrups when I ride.
6. If I ride with my stirrup leathers even, I feel crooked.
7. My upper body tends to twist to one side or the other.
8. My posture could use improvement.
9. I have been diagnosed with scoliosis or vertebral subluxations (misalignment of the spinal column), or I have another known physical condition that causes misalignment when I ride.
10. I have trouble carrying and using a whip in my nondominant hand.

If you answered "true" to any of the items, Numbers 1 to 4, you may need to work on developing equal strength on both sides of your body. If you answered "true" to any of items, Numbers 5 to 9, you may need to address postural flaws, bad position habits, or a structural misalignment. If you answered "true" to item Number 10, you need to develop the ability to use your nondominant hand.

Set Your Goals

In your journal or notebook, write a sentence or two that describes a realistic (30-day) goal regarding your body alignment. Examples:

"I will attain noticeable improvement in the strength of my nondominant side."

"I will learn to feel the difference between sitting with a collapsed hip and sitting evenly, with my weight distributed equally over both seat bones."

"I will become comfortable using the whip in either hand."

Exercises

Proper breathing is very important in facilitating core strength and body alignment and in executing movements, both on the ground and in the saddle.

There are two types of breathers: "chest elevators" and "core breathers." A chest elevator uses the accessory respiratory muscles in the neck and the tops of the shoulders. This type of breathing raises the shoulders and delivers only a limited amount of oxygen—not the ideal, especially for an athlete. In contrast, a core breather inhales using the diaphragm and the core muscles, which allows the shoulders to soften and more oxygen to be taken in. She also uses the diaphragm—which has insertion sites into the core muscles—to facilitate breathing.

The first exercise I'll give you will help you learn core breathing. The second also facilitates core breathing while helping you to straighten and align your body.

EXERCISE 1: Flaring and Funneling the Ribs

To learn core breathing, lie on your back with your knees bent and your palms on your lower ribs. Inhale deeply through your nose, imagining that you are filling your lungs all the way with oxygen; and allow your hands and the ribs beneath to "flare" or expand (fig 6.6 A). Allow your shoulders, head, and neck to relax and soften. As you exhale through your mouth, try to make your lower ribs "funnel" toward one another and down toward your toes (fig. 6.6 B). Practice until you can make your ribs disappear under your hands as you funnel and exhale. Start by using this breathing technique as you axially elongate, and then later use it throughout the day. When you ride, use the core-breathing technique to relax your upper body, to deliver needed oxygen to your hard-working muscles, to align your body in the saddle, and to give yourself greater core control.

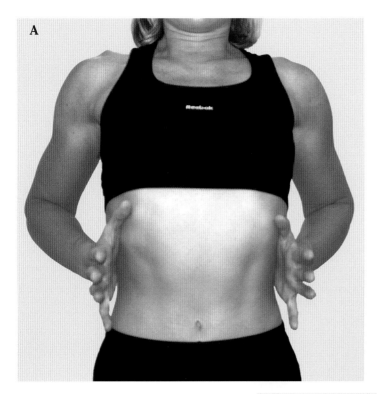

6.6 A & B

Susan "flares" (expands) her ribs by inhaling deeply through her nose and filling her lungs **(A)**.

Here Susan "funnels" her ribs down and toward one another as she exhales deeply through her mouth **(B)**.

The BODY Element: Alignment

What Your Horse Needs to Have

As I've explained, to make your horse straight, you must position him so that, when he works on a single track, his hind feet travel in the same lines as do his forefeet and his spine is parallel to the line of travel. Again, these concepts apply to both travel in a straight line and travel on a circle or turn. Only when a horse is straight can his hind legs carry equal weight and develop equal carrying and pushing power, and these factors are important prerequisites for the sixth and final building block of the *Training Pyramid,* collection.

If your horse is not *aligned* properly, he can't honestly go freely forward. As a result, he may lose the fluidity of his movement, his steps may become irregular, he may carry his topline unevenly (and the topline itself may appear uneven over time due to unequal musculature), he may "fall" onto one shoulder as he travels, and he could possibly drop a hip (drift asymmetrically) as he moves. Over time, these problems may affect his soundness: He may develop a sore back, show signs of soreness in the feet on the side that bears a disproportionate amount of his weight, or display negative behavioral changes.

Assess Your Horse's Skill Level

Is your horse aligned? Many riders already know the ways in which their mounts tend to become crooked. If you're not sure, use the following exercises to assess your horse's degree of straightness.

1. Establish a regular working or collected trot, and proceed in a straight line toward a mirror. (If you lack access to a mirror, ask a knowledgeable helper to stand at one end of the arena. He or she can videotape you if you like.) If your horse is truly straight, his hind legs will not be visible to the sides of his front legs, and his head and neck will be centered directly in front of his chest (fig. 6.11 A).

   Before you reach the mirror or the end of the arena, quietly halt. How many legs can you see? Did he throw his haunches to one side or the other as he halted? Are his head, neck, and chest aligned and centered over his forelegs? Is his head perpendicular to the ground, or is it tilted?

6.11 A – D Crookedness

*Giotto is almost straight with his head slightly to the right **(A)**. He is demonstrating straightness (alignment) on a circle **(B)**. Giotto has lost his straightness at the canter because his shoulders have fallen out. His poll is too deep, my inside leg is pushing him to the left, and my outside leg is not supporting the shoulder. My inside rein is pulling his neck to the inside and the outside rein doesn't support the neck. The result is his neck comes to the inside while his body travels straight **(C)**.*

Crookedness is a sign that one side of your horse's body is stronger (and, usually, tighter) than the other. Because it takes effort for him to bring his hind legs squarely underneath his body, his haunches will tend to drift to the weaker side.

2. Establish a 20-meter circle right in working or collected trot. Ask a helper to stand in the middle of the circle and tell you whether your horse's head, neck, shoulders, and haunches are aligned on the curve of the circle (fig. 6.11 B). (If you don't have access to a knowledgeable helper, ask someone to videotape your ride and analyze it yourself.) Now have your helper stand outside the circle to make the same assessments. Have the shoulders fallen in or "popped out"? Have the haunches fallen in or drifted out (fig. 6.11 C)?

respective disciplines. Many horses are misunderstood, mistreated, confused, frightened, overfaced, bored, neglected, or even abused—often out of ignorance rather than deliberate intent. Such horses cannot possibly be content with their existence.

At the same time, some personalities—both human and equine—do seem more inherently contented than others. So, if your horse is a dyed-in-the-wool grouch, he may never achieve supreme contentment. Still, I believe that there are things that you can do to increase your horse's level of contentment, no matter what his basic personality.

Assess Your Horse's Psyche

How does your horse rank on the contentment scale? Take the following short quiz and find out.

For each item, choose the response that best describes your horse.

1. When I walk into the barn, my horse responds by:
    a) Retreating to the corner of his stall
    b   Pinning his ears
    c) Nickering

2. In the stall, my horse is:
    a) Fearful
    b) Neurotic
    c) Calm and relaxed

3. When I brush and groom my horse, he acts:
    a) Tense and fidgety
    b) Aggressive
    c) Happy to be touched and fussed over

4. When I tack up my horse, he acts:
    a) Resigned
    b) Crabby
    c) Pleased

5. Under saddle, my horse generally is:
    a) Dull
    b) Cranky and irritable
    c) Eager and responsive

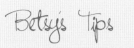

A contented horse has a joy about him—a sense of light-heartedness about what he's doing. When he goes out to work, he's happy and his ears are alert and forward. He eats well.

Contentment stems from peace of mind—and it is difficult for your horse to be contented if you're anxious or upset yourself. Sometimes a quiet walk on the trail can settle both of your minds, as can the realization of how fortunate you are to be spending time with your horse, doing something you love.

If your responses were mostly "a's," your horse may have some fear issues that are preventing him from feeling content with you and his work. If you answered mostly "b's," something or someone may be rubbing him the wrong way. If you answered mostly "c's," he's a pretty happy guy.

Set Your Goals

In your journal or notebook, write a sentence or two that describes a realistic goal regarding your horse's level of contentment. Example:

"To see a marked improvement in his level of contentment after 30 days."

Exercises

Check with a veterinarian, an equine massage therapist, a saddler, and chiropractor to make sure there are no physical causes that may be contributing to your horse's discontent, such as ill-fitting shoes or tack, sore muscles, or misaligned vertebrae.

Next, examine your horse's environment carefully. Does it contain potential irritants? For instance, some horses are sensitive to sound. Does a radio blare all day long? Try turning it down or off and see if your horse's demeanor improves. Does he strongly dislike one of his neighbors? Try putting him or the offending neighbor in a different stall. Is the amount of activity outside his stall to his liking? Some horses are busybodies who enjoy monitoring the goings-on in the barn; others get irritated or excited by the constant parade of people, horses, and dogs past their doors and are much calmer and happier when housed in a quieter part of the barn.

Finally, evaluate your own riding as a source of potential irritants. If you wear spurs, are they too strong for your horse's sensitive sides? Do you drive too hard and too long with your legs without releasing while you ride? Do your legs and heels bang his sides incessantly because you have trouble keeping them still? Are you prone to losing your balance and catching him in the mouth? Do you get so caught up in the work that you forget to allow him to walk and rest periodically—or, when you do give him a break, do you keep holding and driving, even in the walk?

Progress Check

A contented horse is relaxed and happy after his workouts. When you're done riding, does your horse really relax, stretch out, and walk comfortably on long reins?

ANSWERS TO QUESTIONS ON PAGE 181

The correct answer to each item is "b."

7.1
In **COLLECTION**, the haunches lower and carry more weight, allowing lightness and freedom in the forehand.

CHAPTER SEVEN

Building Block 6: *Collection*

Collection (kə lek′shən), *n.*
1. the act of collecting.
2. something that is collected, as a group of objects or an amount of material accumulated in one location, esp. for some purpose or as a result of some process.

ollection is the final building block of the training scale and one that even expert riders on experienced horses work to develop and hone throughout their mounts' careers. In his book *Basic Training of the Young Horse*, Dr. Reiner Klimke explains the concept of collection as follows:

> *Collection entails putting more weight onto the hind legs through the lowering of the quarters and hocks which enables the horse to use its full potential strength. The more weight there is on the hind legs the freer are the shoulders and therefore the easier it is for the horse to shift its point of balance backwards. This is important not only for dressage but equally for jumping and cross country, for example when taking off for a jump.[1]*

In *The Dressage Horse*, Harry Boldt explains how to use the aids to achieve collection:

> *…by using simultaneous half halts and driving aids to push the horse more together and "through," thus allowing the weight to be transferred more onto the quarters, the horse then becomes collected.*
>
> *So the hand of the rider therefore acts on the quarters, but only together with a forward pushing back and leg aids, which encourage the hind legs to step powerfully under the body.*
>
> *Through the increased loading the quarters have to work harder, and*

---

[1] *USDF Manual*, p. 158. Reprinted with permission of J. A. Allen.

through this the three joints of hip, stifle and hock become more gymnastic. The quarters are lowered and correspondingly the forehand is raised.

The more flexible the quarters the more the steps and spring of the horse gain expression.

He has, through the lifting of the forehand, now only a very fine contact with the rider's hand.

The greatest mistake a rider can make in collecting his horse is too strong a use of the hand without the simultaneous forward push of the back and leg. Through this the steps will become shorter but not more expressive. Eventually the purity of the paces will suffer.

The pushing aids must therefore ensure that the Schwung remains during collection. This will lead to a greater improvement in "throughness," with the horse accepting the aids without faltering. The Schwung in the quarters goes through to the mouth whilst the rein aids, in combination with back and leg aids, move through to the quarters.[2]

As you can see from the above descriptions, collection involves the horse's entire body. It is a misconception to think that collection begins and ends with the horse's high head carriage and profile on the vertical. However, if you try to bring your horse's head and neck up into a collected "frame" before he has developed the correct musculature throughout his body, it will be difficult for him to support his head and neck in that posture. That's why head carriage should be viewed as a result of the correct development of the horse, not as an end in and of itself; and that's why *gymnastic training* is done through progressive body building and supporting stages. Children have to learn algebra before they can grasp geometry, and they must know the concepts and logic of geometry before they can progress to understanding calculus. Your horse's physical development works the same way. Trying to put a horse into a frame he's not prepared to carry is like planting a seed, then standing over the ground demanding that it grow—now! The seed will grow if you give it time and provide it the right environment, but you can't willfully rush its development.

2 *USDF Manual,* pp. 161-162. Reprinted with permission of Edition Haberbeck.

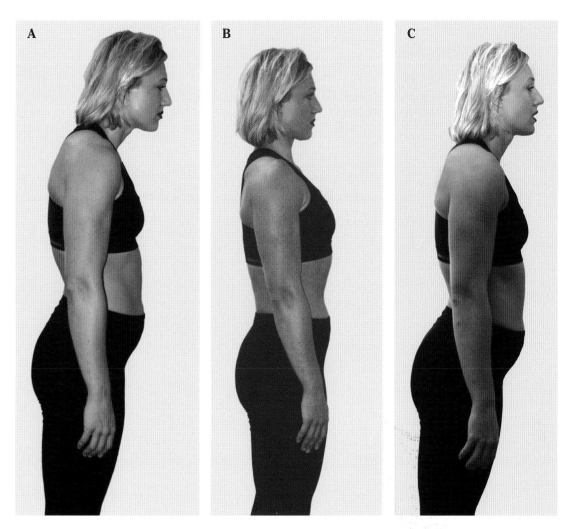

A   B   C

**7.2 A — C
Posture**
This posture is unattractive; it'll also make you ineffective in the saddle and unable to create power. If you were to ride in this posture, your horse might well be on his forehand and with his haunches trailing out behind **(A)**.

This strong, elegant posture puts you in control, both on the ground and in the saddle. Susan's ears are over her shoulders, her shoulder blades are back and squared, her lower ribs are funneled and drawn in, her core is engaged, and her pelvis is in a neutral position. Her entire body is empowered **(B)**.

Compare the photos 7.2 (A) and (B) above. The poor-posture stance includes an anterior head carriage (with the head carried forward and not aligned with the shoulders). This posture causes the shoulders and upper back to round, which weakens the shoulder-blade and anterior neck muscles. Over time, the strain of this position causes the *pectoralis major* chest muscle to shorten, thus forcing the shoulders to remain rounded. In addition, the muscles that hold the shoulder blades back and keep the shoulders square become stretched and weak. This scenario is known as *upper-cross syndrome*. Not only is upper-cross syndrome visually unappealing; it also decreases your ability to maintain core control and to develop sufficient functional strength in your upper extremities. What s more, if

Hyperlordosis—an accentuated curve in the lower back—as seen here, is a common postural fault. A soft lumbar curve (lordosis) as seen in in 7.2 B, is proper lower-body posture **(C)**.

you ride in this posture, your horse may mirror your "on the forehand" position by lowering his head and neck.

For proper upper-body posture, the upper spine must be able to flatten instead of rounding forward. Flexible pectoralis major muscles and functionally strong scapular retractors hold the shoulder blades toward each other. Finally, strong muscles at the front of the neck hold the head in place, with the opening of the ears over the tops of the shoulders.

If there is any extraneous uncontrolled movement in your hip and pelvic region or in your lower back, your upper body, head, and neck will reflect the movement (the unattractive head-bobbing seen in many dressage riders, particularly at the sitting trot).

Proper lower-body posture includes a soft lumbar curve in the lower back (*lordosis*), which places the pelvis in a neutral position. A common postural fault is an accentuated curve in the lower back called *hyperlordosis* (fig. 7.2 C). This places the pelvis in an anterior (forward) position, which causes the upper legs to rotate outward—a disadvantage for riders, who need to rotate their thighs inward to achieve an effective position in the saddle. Hyperlordosis also causes the abdominal muscles to protrude, thus disengaging the core, causing the lower-back muscles to shorten and tighten, and limiting the range of movement of the hip flexors. This scenario is known as *lower-cross syndrome*.

As with upper-cross syndrome, lower-cross syndrome is visually unappealing and decreases the rider's ability to maintain core control. It also decreases the capacity for functional strength in the lower extremities. It can also lead to unwanted head-bobbing or shoulder movement.

7.3
Posterior Deltoid Exercise
As I sit on an exercise ball holding two small dumbbells, I extend my arms back behind me, keeping my shoulder blades down and toward each other.

EXERCISE 1: For the Posterior Deltoids

For this exercise, you'll need an exercise ball and two small dumbbells (no heavier than five pounds each).

Sit on the ball with your knees level with your hips and your ankles under your knees. Axially elongate and draw in your core. Hold the dumbbells with your arms at your sides and your palms facing behind you. Inhale; exhale and lift your arms back behind you while keeping your shoulder blades down and toward each other. Don't shrug or lift your shoulders as you lift your arms. Inhale and lower your arms back to your sides (fig. 7.3). Do ten repetitions.

7.4 A – C
Canter Departs
Susan assists by holding a loop of stretch tubing as I sit on an exercise ball, my arms in riding position and holding the handles at the ends of the loop **(A)**.

EXERCISE 2: Canter Departs

This exercise requires a partner. Sit on the ball in the position described in Exercise 1. Have your partner hold the end of a loop of stretch tubing, and hold the ends of the tubing as if you were holding a pair of reins, with your arms in riding position. Sit with your pelvis in neutral position. Tilt your pelvis into a posterior pelvic tilt. Keeping your arms still, pull your body forward toward your arms, allowing your arms to bend at the elbows. The movement mimics the canter aids and will help give you the correct feel for the canter depart (figs. 7.4 A – C). Do five repetitions.

In a movement that's similar to the aid for a canter depart, I use my core muscles to pull my body forward toward my arms. I am not using my arm muscles to initiate the forward movement (**B**).

Ending position for the canter-depart exercise. I've used my core muscles to roll the ball back to where I started. This action mimics following the motion of the canter with your seat (**C**).

7.5

Single Leg Stretch

While engaging my core muscles and lifting my shoulder blades off the floor, I've placed my right hand beside my bent left knee and my left hand alongside my left ankle. I'll switch hand positions as I switch legs, all the while keeping the straight leg from touching the floor.

EXERCISE 3: Single Leg Stretch

Lie on your back with your right knee lifted into your chest and your left leg straight and raised off the floor. Using your core muscles, roll up, lifting your shoulders off the floor and keeping your chin between your shoulders and your breastbone. Exhale and reach your right hand to your right ankle while placing your left hand on top of your left knee. Inhale and switch legs; exhale and reach your left hand to your left ankle and your right hand to your right knee. With each exhalation, draw in your core and lift your sternum (fig. 7.5). Do ten repetitions.

EXERCISE 4: The Hundred—Breathing

Lie on your back with your arms at your sides and your knees bent; later, for an additional challenge, try keeping your legs straight. Roll up, raising your shoulders off the floor and keeping your chin between your shoulders and over your breastbone. Begin pumping your arms; the movement comes from the shoulders while the arms stay straight. Inhale for a count of five while pumping your arms, and exhale for a count of five while pumping your arms. Repeat the sequence ten times, for a total of a hundred (thus the name of this exercise). As you inhale, think about keeping your breastbone and shoulders raised. As you exhale, draw in your core (figs. 7.6 A – D).

7.6 A – D

The Hundred

Starting position for the Hundred. I'm engaging my core muscles to lift my head, neck, and shoulders instead of straining my neck forward **(A)**.

How high you'll roll up off the floor in the Hundred depends in part on how flexible your spine is. My spine is not very flexible, as you can see from this photo—my back is practically flat **(B)**.

Compare the previous photo with this shot of Susan doing the same exercise. Her spine is much more flexible than mine, which enables her to keep her shoulder blades closer to the floor as she rolls up **(C)**.

This photo shows a more advanced position for the Hundred: Susan extends her legs straight up toward the ceiling as she pumps her arms. Her spine remains rounded, and her shoulder blades are off the ground **(D)**.

7.7 A & B
The Quadruped

Starting position for the Quadruped. My thighs and arms are perpendicular to the ground, my back is flat, and I'm keeping my head and neck aligned with my spine (A).

By lifting and extending my opposite arm and leg, I'm really testing my core stability alignment. My form in this photo is okay, but ideally I'd like to see my right leg, back, neck, and left arm form a straight line (B).

EXERCISE 5: The Quadruped

Get down on the floor on all fours, with your shoulders over your wrists and your knees under your hips. Draw in your core so that your back flattens like a table top. Look down toward the floor so that your neck does not arch back. Exhale and reach your right arm in front of you; inhale and lower your arm. Repeat the sequence with your left arm; then try lifting your legs one at a time while keeping your hands on the ground. Keep your hips stable and your core engaged—don't let your back sag. After you feel confident lifting your arms and legs singly, try raising your right arm and your left leg together; then lift your left arm and your right leg. This is a real test of core stability and body alignment. Keep your hips and shoulders level, and make sure that your back does not twist or arch and that you do not drop your hips or shoulders (figs. 7.7 A & B). Do five repetitions of each movement.

7.8 A & B

Posterior Deltoid Exercise

Starting position for the posterior-del-toid exercise on the reformer. I'm kneeling on the carriage, upper body straight, and holding a loop in each hand **(A)**.

Keeping my arms straight, I extend both arms as far behind me as I can without lifting my shoulder blades or leaning with my upper body **(B)**.

For the Advanced Pilates Student: Work on the Reformer

EXERCISE 6: Posterior Deltoid Exercise on the Reformer

Kneel on the carriage with the fronts of your thighs against the shoulder pads. Axially elongate, engage your core, and slide your shoulders down. Hold on to the handles with your palms facing back and your arms by your sides. Inhale; exhale and raise your arms up behind you. Inhale and lower your arms back to your sides. Don't shrug your shoulders, and be careful not to fall forward as the carriage moves (7.8 A & B). This exercise requires a lot of balance! Do ten repetitions.

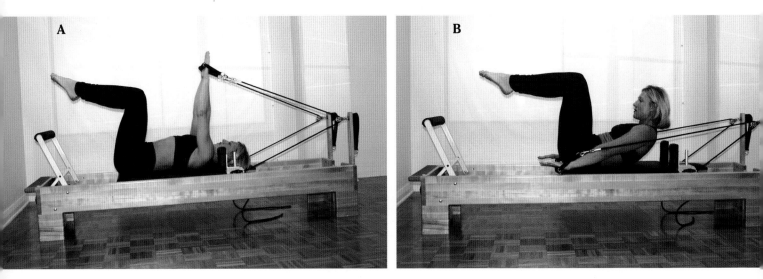

7.9 A & B

The Hundred on the Reformer

Susan demonstrates the starting position for the Hundred on the reformer. Her thighs are parallel to her straight arms, and her core muscles are engaged **(A)**.

Susan has her arms lowered to her sides, ready to begin pumping her arms for the Hundred **(B)**.

EXERCISE 7: The Hundred on the Reformer

Lie on the reformer with your head in the headrest and your arms reaching long, pulling your shoulders away from the shoulder rest and taking your shoulders away from your ears. Establish a neutral pelvis and engage your core. Exhale and raise your knees over your hips. With your arms extended over your head, hold the handles of the pulleys and lower your arms to the carriage, raising your head, neck, and shoulders. Hold the handles with your wrists positioned over your shoulders. Exhale and raise your knees over your hips. Inhale through your nose; exhale through your mouth while funneling your ribs; breathe for a count of 5 while pumping your arms up and down (about 8 inches); and exhale for a count of 5, pumping your arms. The 5 by 5 count equals 10. Do this count 10 times for account of 100 (figs. 7.9 A & B). For an advanced challenge, straighten your legs and point your toes toward the ceiling instead of bending your knees. Do ten repetitions.

EXERCISE 8: Standing Lunge on the Reformer

Stand beside the reformer with your right heel against the shoulder rest, the toes of your right foot resting on the carriage, and your right knee off the carriage. Your left foot is on the floor with the leg straight. Rest your hands on the footbar with your wrists in a neutral position and shoulder blades drawn down your spine. Draw in your core; exhale and press your right leg back, moving only the reformer, until your leg is straight. Feel as if your hips are hinges. Keep both legs straight until you feel a comfortable stretch in your left hamstring. Then continue stretching your leg

7.10 A – D
Standing Lunge
Starting position for the standing lunge. My right foot is resting on the carriage of the reformer, I'm resting my hands on the footbar, and my left leg is on the floor **(A)**. *Beginning lunge: I've pressed my right leg back to achieve a stretch in my right hip flexor, taking care to keep my hips from twisting* **(B)**. *After you gain more flexibility in your hip joint, you'll be able to extend your leg farther back behind you in the standing-lunge exercise, as I'm doing here…* **(C)** *…and eventually far back enough that your leg is parallel to the floor* **(D)**.

backward, bending your left knee and making sure that your knee stays aligned with your left ankle, until you feel a stretch in the hip-flexor muscle of your right hip. Return to the starting position while inhaling and keeping your core engaged. Don't allow your back to arch or your shoulder blades to slide up toward your ears. Do four repetitions with each leg (figs. 7.10 A – D).

7.11 A & B

Kneeling Lunge

Starting position for the kneeling lunge. Keep your hands on your hips and your hips aligned and even **(A)**.

I've pressed my left leg back as far as I comfortably can to stretch my right hamstring. I'm taking care to keep my back straight and my core muscles engaged **(B)**.

EXERCISE 9: Kneeling Lunge on the Reformer

Place your right knee on the carriage with your right heel resting on the shoulder pad and your toes on the carriage. Rest your left heel on the footbar with your left knee directly over your left ankle (runner's lunge position). Draw in your core and axially elongate, bringing your hips forward without arching your back. Exhale and push your right leg back as far as you can comfortably to achieve a stretch in your left hamstring. Try to not round your back as you stretch. Inhale and lead forward with your hips, axially elongating as the carriage returns to the starting position and stretching the front of your hip. Do five repetitions on each side (figs. 7.11 A & B).

Exercises That Mimic Dressage-Specific Movements

The following two exercises were designed to mimic dressage movements, to aid in developing the strength, balance, and coordination necessary to perfect the body movements used while riding. You'll need two exercise discs for these exercises (available from fitness-equipment suppliers).

EXERCISE 10: Kneeling Abduction on Discs

Place one disc on the reformer and one on the footplate. Kneel with one knee on each disc, and rotate your hips inward to riding position. Axially elongate and draw in your core. Inhale; exhale and press the carriage away, trying to keep your knees turned toward each other. Inhale and bring the carriage back to the starting position, maintaining the inward hip rotation. Switch knee positions and repeat the exercise. Do five repetitions in each position (figs. 7.12 A & B).

7.12 A & B

Kneeling Abduction on Discs

Starting position for the kneeling abduction on discs. I'm kneeling with one knee on each disc, one of which is on the reformer carriage and the other of which is on the footplate. My hips are rotated inward to riding position **(A)**.

I've used my abductors (outer thigh muscles) to press the carriage away, maintaining the inward rotation of my hips **(B)**.

7.13 A – C

Half-Pass on Discs

Starting position for the half-pass on discs. My hands are on one disc and my knees are on the other. My back is flat, my core muscles are engaged, my head and neck are aligned with my spine, and my arms and thighs are perpendicular to the floor **(A)**.

A

EXERCISE 11: Half-Pass on Discs

For fun, try this exercise to feel what your horse feels when asked to bend and flex. This exercise, which mimics the half-pass movement, will help you to better understand how your core affects your upper and lower body.

Place both hands on one disc and both knees on the other disc. Axially elongate and draw in your core so that your back is flat. Turn your head and your shoulders to the right. Feel what happens to your hips: They turn to the right, too. Then turn your head and your shoulders to the left and feel your hips turn to the left. To help facilitate this movement, use your obliques (the abdominal muscles that wrap around the sides) to help you turn in either direction (figs. 7.13 A – C).

Progress Check

Would a spectator say to you, "Boy, it doesn't look as if you're doing anything"? If an observer can't see what you're doing, you're definitely on the right track.

Here's an another good indicator of progress: Even though you're really working, the riding doesn't seem difficult. You have a strong sense of clarity. Ask your-

Progress Check

Use the exercise from *Assess Your Horse's Understanding* on page 237 as your benchmark for determining whether your horse's balance has improved.

…and here he is after I release the reins. He's tipped slightly onto his forehand, but overall he's remained round and balanced **(B)**.

The BODY Element: Self-Carriage

What Your Horse Needs to Have

Self-carriage is considered the *ne plus ultra* of collection. As the German National Equestrian Federation explains,

> *When the horse is correctly trained, his neck shapes itself. The lowering of the quarters determines how high the neck is carried and arched; the horse*

carries itself. Whereas if the head and neck position are created by the reins mainly or solely, the rider has to carry the horse's head and neck with his hands.

If the carrying capacity of the quarters is developed sufficiently, the horse is able to carry his own and his rider's weight in perfect balance.[4]

The Fédération Equestre Internationale (FEI) concurs with the German Federation's explanation of self-carriage. The FEI Handbook states that an "acceptable collection" is "characterized by ease and carriage" as well as by impulsion[5].

When a horse is in self-carriage, riding becomes nearly effortless because the horse is not relying on his rider to "hold him together" or to push him forward. He is moving in total balance and offering the movements as of his own accord. It is at this level of training that the horse looks as if he is dancing.

Assess Your Horse's Skill Level

In its official handbook, the German National Equestrian Federation describes a surefire way to determine whether your horse is moving in self-carriage:

To examine whether a horse is in balance or not, the rider can be asked to "give and retake" the reins [an exercise dubbed descente de main by the classical master François Robichon de la Guérinière[6]], as is done in some dressage tests. Then, for a few strides, the rider has to give up the contact, which anyway at this stage of training is only light. Momentarily, without any contact, a balanced horse will not change tempo nor change his head and neck carriage. This is in contrast to the exercise described earlier [the "stretching circle"], where the young horse, given the reins, follows them by lowering his head and lengthening his neck.[7]

If you give the reins for a few strides and the tempo or your horse's head and neck position changes or he falls out of balance, you will know that he is not in self-carriage.

Set Your Goals

In your journal or notebook, write a sentence or two that describes a realistic goal regarding the attainment of self-carriage. Example:

"Within 30 days, I will strengthen my horse so that I can increase the number of strides in which he can maintain self-carriage when I release the reins."

4 *USDF Manual,* p. 173. From *Principles of Riding: The Official Handbook of the German National Equestrian Federation.* Reprinted with permission of Half Halt Press.

5 *USDF Manual,* p. 265.

6 *USDF Manual,* p. 261.

7 *USDF Manual,* p. 173. Reprinted with permission of Half Halt Press.

Exercise

EXERCISE: Developing Carrying Power

The goal of this exercise is to teach your horse to adjust his gaits smoothly and promptly (to go "forward and back" within each gait). Doing so will help him to establish the power and lift needed for collection. When he is collected, he moves with *carrying power*: a light forehand, lift in his strides, and his inside hind leg causing the energy to move forward up to the bridle (fig. 7.15).

Begin the exercise by establishing a regular and rhythmic working or collected trot on a 20-meter circle at A. (For this exercise, let's assume that you're on the left rein.) On the circle, bring your horse's forehand to the inside as you think of a haunches-out-like positioning. From that haunches-out-like positioning, change to shoulder-in *without the shoulder's changing position*; only the head and neck positioning and the body bend change, and even these changes are very slight. It requires extreme concentration on the rider's part to go from haunches-out to shoulder-in while keeping the horse's shoulders the same. Keep your hands light as you ride through this exercise, thinking of pushing the activity of the hind legs forward and up into the contact of the reins (fig. 7.16 A).

Next, trot down the long side of the arena (from F to M) in haunches-out, changing your horse's positioning to shoulder-in by the middle of the long side. Support him with your outside upper leg and knee to make sure that his outside shoulder doesn't "drop" to the outside. Straighten him before the corner, and ride through the corner in correct left bend.

7.15
Haunches-out (renvers) is an excellent exercise for developing collection.

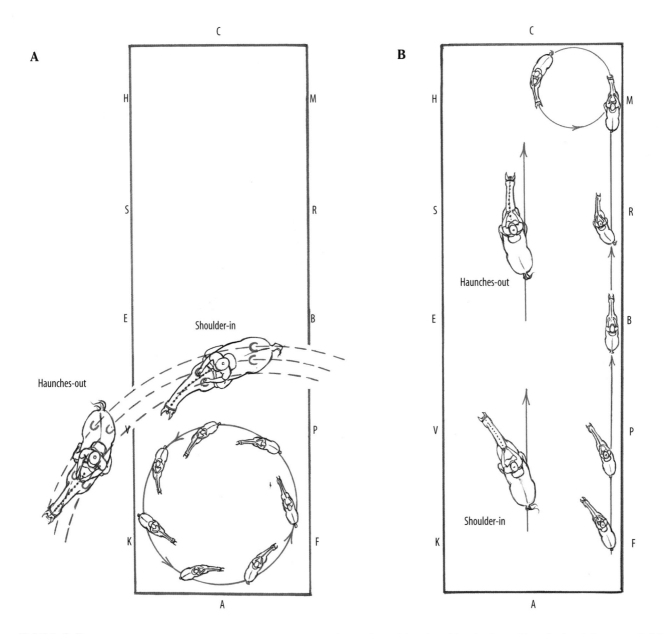

7.16 A & B
Develop Carrying Power
The first part of the exercise to develop carrying power supples your horse **(A)**. *On the long sides, the quick change from haunches-out to medium trot will help the horse collect his body. The whole exercise develops the horse and gives him more lift and cadence* **(B)**.

Along the next long side, ride shoulder-in from H to S. Straighten and ride forward in medium trot from S to V. At V, collect and ride haunches-out. At K, make a ten-meter circle; ride five or six strides of the circle in a slight haunches-out positioning to ensure straightness, then return to correct left bend on the circle.

On the next long side (F to M), repeat the sequence of movements: shoulder-in from F to P; straighten and medium trot from P to R; collect and haunches-out at R; 10-meter circle at M, working with haunches-out positioning to normal bend (7.16 B).

As you ride through this portion of the exercise, aim for lift and greater cadence. Ride the ten-meter circle with a slight outside flexion for a stride or two—a "touch" into both reins, followed immediately by a release. The "touch"—or a squeezing of the reins—is a half-halt that gets your horse's attention and focuses him on whichever aid you're using the most. It's used similarly to the way you might tap someone on the shoulder and then direct his or her attention by pointing your finger—a sort of "Hey! Pay attention here!"

After you have ridden through the entire exercise on the left rein, repeat the sequence on the right rein and then give the exercise a try in both directions at the canter.

Progress Check

Use the *descente de main* exercise from *Assess Your Horse's Skill Level,* page 240, as the progress check for this component. If your horse starts out unable to maintain his balance, rhythm, and tempo when you give the reins but can do so for a few strides after 30 days of practicing the above exercises, you've made excellent progress.

In contrast, a feeling of lightness in the hand often indicates a dropping-off of the connection—a lack of completion of the "circle of aids" or the "muscle ring." True connection—genuine self-carriage—feels constant throughout the horse's body.

The SPIRIT Element: Focus

What Your Horse Needs to Be

You, the rider, are not the only one who needs to be "in the zone" in order to achieve a performance characterized by ease, grace, and harmony. Your horse, too, has to be 100 percent focused on his work and on you.

A horse's ability to *focus* is determined in part by his basic temperament. As Dr. Reiner Klimke notes in *Basic Training of the Young Horse,*

> The horse is born with its temperament and physique. We can improve both with the right education and environment....On the other hand, the reverse can happen if wrong and bad handling is practised. The faults with which the horse is born and acquires are difficult to correct. Experience teaches

Betsy's Tips

Self-carriage should feel easy—although to path to self-carriage may not always be easy! You feel as if you're part of the horse. True self-carriage means that the line of energy comes from behind, over the topline, and through the neck, reaching forward to the hands; the horse isn't made light by being pulled back. The feeling of riding a horse that's moving in self-carriage is "upward, lift, out toward the hand into connection."

that even after patient and hard work faults can reappear in a horse when an opportunity presents itself.[8]

Nervous horses tend to have the most difficulty focusing, as their excitable natures make them susceptible to distractions and tension. Klimke writes, "Nervous horses tend to take flight when faced with unusual situations such as strange noises, quick movements and flags....It is my experience that a horse with this characteristic will never completely lose its nervousness. The trainer just has to accept the limitations."[9]

Of course, just because a horse is not nervous does not necessarily mean that he is focused on his work. For instance, most of us have ridden lazy horses who expended a great deal of brainpower in figuring out ways to get out of working. For a horse to be focused on his work, he must possess all the "spirit" elements of the earlier building blocks: *obedience and work ethic*, *willingness*, *trust* and *confidence*, an *"electric" mindset*, and *contentment*. He is happy and relaxed, he knows and likes his job, he is eager to please his rider, and he wants to work.

Although some horses inherently can focus on their work better than others, the quality of focus can be developed. Here's how.

Assess Your Horse's Psyche

How well does your horse focus? Take the following quiz to find out.

1. Does your horse tend to be spooky and skittish, even after he's warmed up?
2. Is he inclined to try one evasion after another instead of putting in an honest effort?
3. When he is in the schooling or show ring, is his demeanor "all business"?
4. Does he seem so attuned to your wishes that you need do little more than "think" what you want him to do and he does it?
5. Is he inclined to pay more attention to other horses than he does to you?

If you answered yes to questions 1, 2, and 5 and no to questions 3 and 4, focus is not your horse's strong suit. In the next sections, I'll give you some strategies for helping him to improve his focus.

---

8 *USDF Manual,* p. 310. Reprinted with permission of J. A. Allen.

9 Ibid.

Set Your Goals

In your journal or notebook, write a sentence or two that describes a realistic goal regarding your horse's ability to focus on his work. Examples:

"Within 30 days, to notice a marked increase in my horse's concentration while I'm riding."

"To change the majority of his psychological energy from 'trying to get out of work' to 'concentrating on his job.'"

Exercise

If your horse loses his focus, do an exercise that forces him to concentrate. If he gets distracted, increase the pressure from your seat to draw his attention to you. If he looks right, flex him left. Do something to get his attention. If you're in the show ring when he gets distracted, use the corners to keep his attention coming back to you. Use your aids to keep a conversation going; he can't wander from your conversation.

Check the precision of your aids to improve your horse's focus. If he becomes inattentive, keep him busy by changing his balance (e.g., by making transitions) or by changing directions (e.g., by doing lateral movements).

Progress Check

You'll know that your horse's focus has improved if you see noticeable improvement in those areas in which his focus tends to wander: spookiness, reacting to the presence of other horses, expending energy in ways other than work. Ask yourself: Does he demonstrate heightened awareness of your seat and aids? Are his responses to your aids very clear?

Summary

Congratulations! I admire your dedicated commitment to this program. You have done some serious work and now should have a good grasp of what it takes to reach the top of the *Classical Training Pyramid.* You've also learned some helpful strategies for addressing the issues of your horse's and your own mind, body, and spirit. I hope that this systematic, detailed look at the intellectual, physical, and psychological elements that make up each of my Mind-Body-Spirit Building Blocks has

Betsy's Tips

Keep your horse concentrating on you through the correct use of your seat and aids. If he loses focus, check to see whether you also have lost focus. If he is distracted, have you become distracted?

helped you to gain a deeper understanding of what's involved in attaining an abiding and satisfying partnership with your horse—and a renewed appreciation for the time, energy, hard work, wise decisions, and good judgment that go into the development of a complete equine performer. I also hope that I have helped you to understand how important it is for you to devote the time and energy to your own training as a rider and athlete. Perhaps you'll find that you not only feel better when you ride, but you'll also feel stronger and healthier in all aspects of your life. Over my many years of working with horses and riders, it has become clear to me that the more in tune the rider is with her own body, the more empathy she has toward her horse, the more understanding she has of the training process, and the better results she is able to achieve.

I hope that this book has been able to answer some questions you may have had about your horse or yourself as athletes, and empowered you to make steady, successful progress. I hope that I've helped you to gain a better understanding of the individual building blocks of the training pyramid, their importance, and their essential nature as part of the foundation of correct training. I also hope that I've helped you to see how essential the "other two-thirds"—the intellectual and spiritual elements for both horse and rider—are in helping to lay that foundation.

How beautifully the Greek horseman, Xenophon, put it when he wrote, "When a horse is induced by a man to assume all the airs and graces that he puts on of himself when he is showing off voluntarily, the result is a horse that likes to be ridden, that presents a magnificent sight, that looks alert, that is the most observed by all observers."[10] When assuming the responsibility to "induce" and "direct" our horses, how very skilled we must be in mind, body, and spirit to "become one" with our horses and to allow them to "appear joyous and magnificent, proud and remarkable for having been ridden"!

I hope that I can help you to establish a connection with that noble and generous animal, the horse.

---

10 Xenophon, *The Art of Horsemanship,* p. 56.
Reprinted with permission of J.A. Allen.

Website Resources

Dr. Hilary Clayton: www.cvm.msu.edu/dressage/thechair.htm
www.equilates.com
www.klassickur.com
www.pilates-studio.com
www.usdf.org
www.yogazone.com